1 Using complete circuits

Making and using electricity

Electricity is an important part of our everyday lives. Electricity is a form of **energy**.

It can be made in different ways: by a **battery**, a **dynamo**, a **generator** and by **static charges**. It can also be made from light, from heat, from certain crystals, from gases and even from fruit.

The photographs show examples of the different ways in which we use electrical energy. Some use a battery. Others use the mains electricity supply which comes into our homes and work places.

Q1 Copy this table.

Uses a battery	*Uses the mains supply*
A personal stereo	

Q2 A personal stereo uses a battery. What energy sources do the other devices use? Complete the table.

Q3 There are many electrical devices which you use in the home and at school. Add them to your list.

Extension exercise 1 can be used now.

The complete circuit

Let's see what happens when you connect a battery to a bulb.

Q1 Copy this table.

Material	*Bulb on (✓) or off (✗)*
copper strip	

Safety Warning
In this book you will make safe circuits which use a low voltage. Never experiment with the mains electricity: it is dangerous and can kill.

Apparatus

- ☐ 1.5V battery ☐ battery holder
- ☐ 1.25V bulb ☐ bulb holder
- ☐ small screwdriver
- ☐ pieces of the following materials: copper, iron, steel, brass, plastic, rubber, wood, aluminium ☐ crocodile clips
- ☐ 3 connecting wires

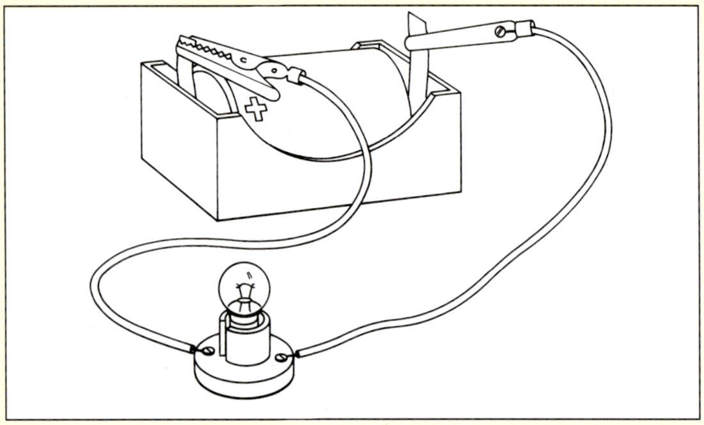

A Build this **circuit**. Connect a battery to a bulb. ▲

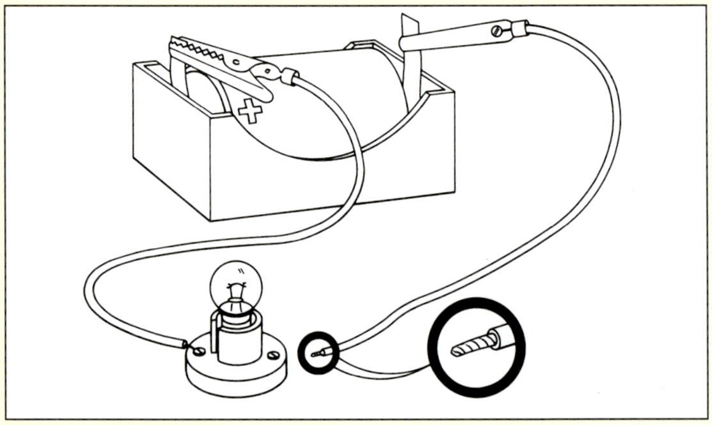

B Now make a gap in your circuit by undoing one of the connecting wires. ▲

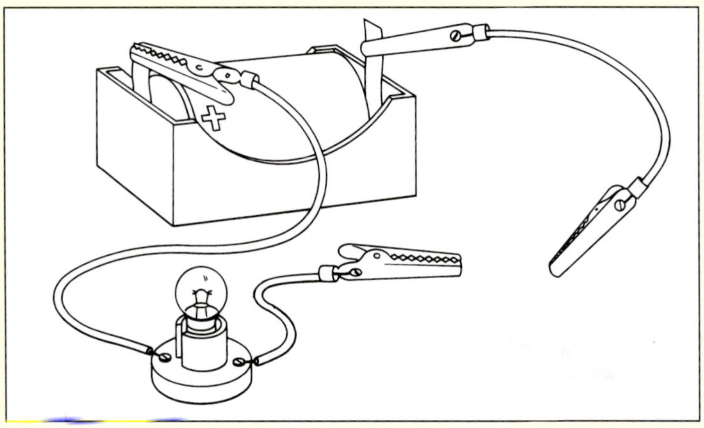

C Build this circuit. Connect crocodile clips to the ends of the connecting wires. ▲

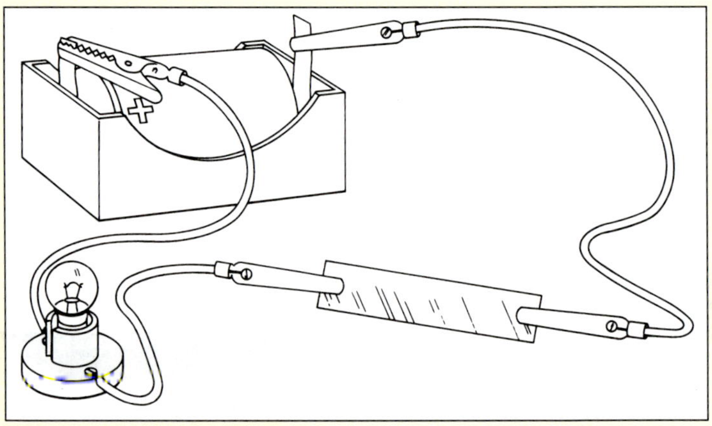

D Connect your materials between the two crocodile clips. Record your results in the table. ▲

All electrical circuits must be complete. If there is a break or a gap nothing will happen. Materials which allow the bulb to light are called **conductors.** The ones which do not are called **insulators**.

Q2 What happens to the bulb in **A**?

Q3 What happens to the bulb when there is a gap in the circuit?

Q4 Which materials, when connected across the gap, made the bulb light up?

Q5 Which materials, when connected across the gap, did not light the bulb?

2 Voltage and current

Apparatus

- ☐ 2 × 1.5 V batteries
- ☐ 2 battery holders ☐ 2.5 V bulb
- ☐ bulb holder
- ☐ small screwdriver
- ☐ 3 connecting wires
- ☐ low voltage buzzer
- ☐ crocodile clips

More volts

In this experiment you are going to find out what happens to a bulb when you use more batteries to increase the **voltage**.

A Build this circuit. Observe the brightness of the bulb. ▼

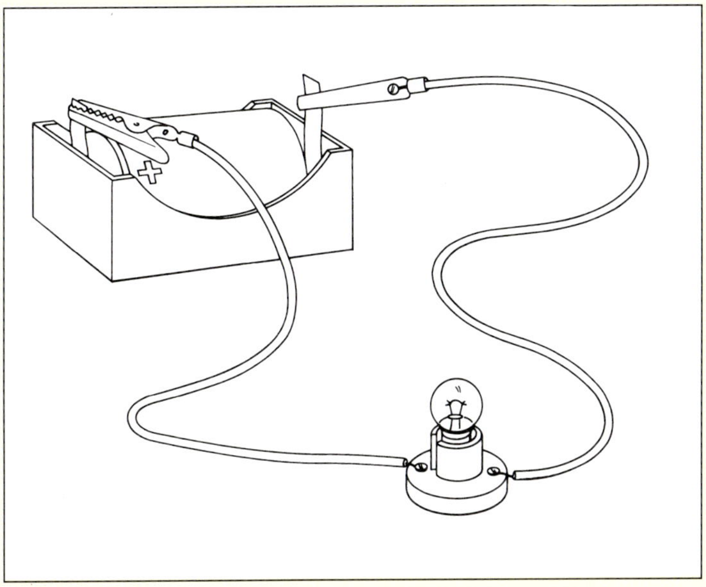

B Build this circuit. Observe the brightness of the bulb. ▼

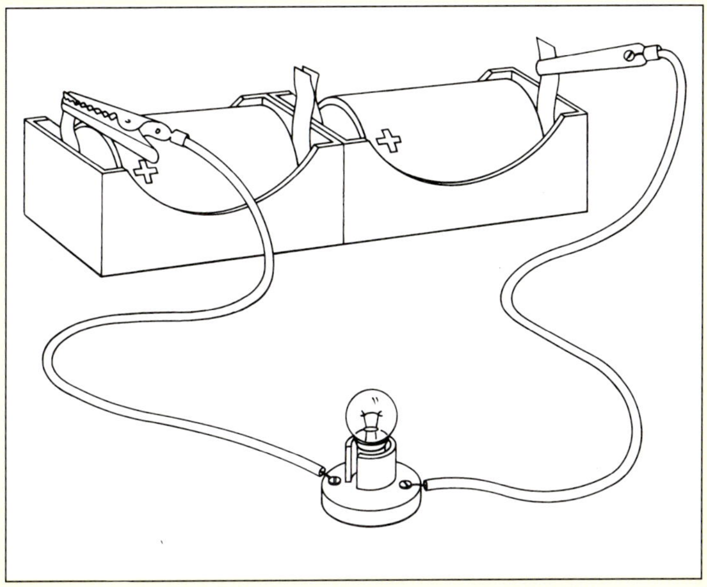

C Build this circuit. Listen to the buzzer. ▼

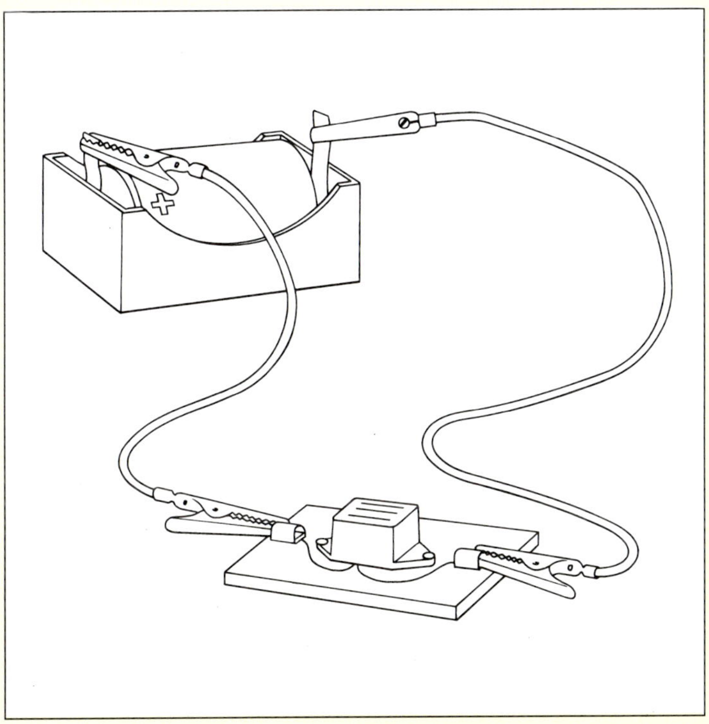

D Build this circuit. Listen to the buzzer. ▼

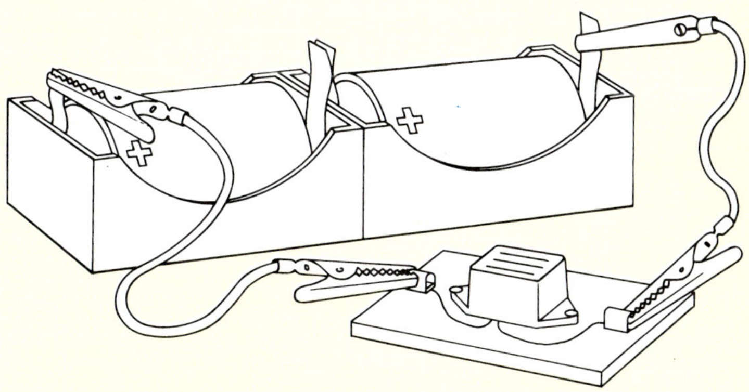

Q1 What happens to the bulb when you use two batteries?

Q2 What happens to the buzzer when you use two batteries?

Q3 What do you think would happen to an electric motor if you increased the voltage?

Controlling the current with resistors

The variable resistor

A variable resistor can be used to control how much **current** flows through an electrical device. An example is the volume control on a radio.

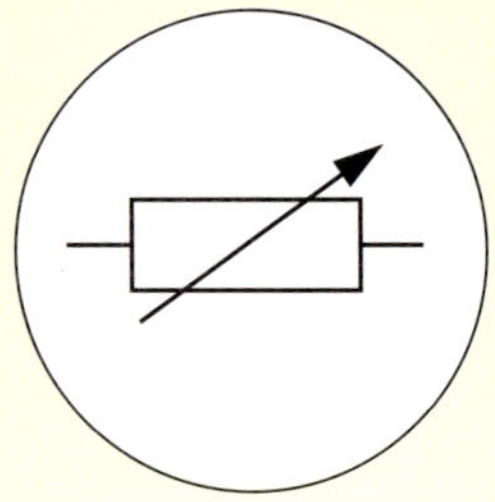

Apparatus	
☐ 2 × 1.5V batteries	☐ bulb holder
☐ 2 battery holders	☐ 2.5V bulb
☐ crocodile clips	
☐ small screwdriver	
☐ 0–25 ohm variable resistor	
☐ 3 connecting wires	
☐ low voltage electric motor	

In this experiment you are going to use a **variable resistor** to control the amount of current flowing through a circuit.

A Build this circuit. ▼

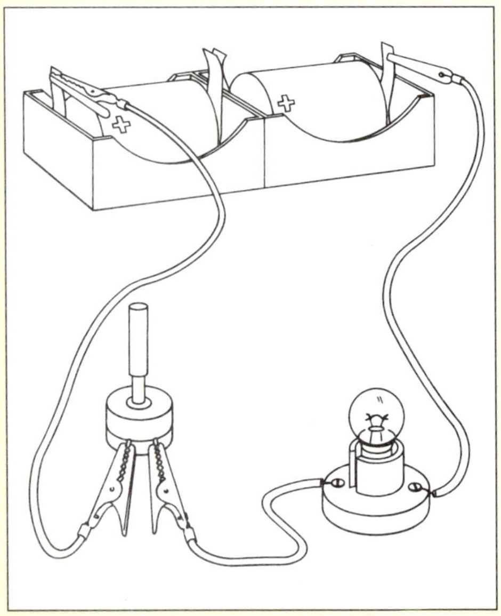

B Adjust the variable resistor and observe what happens to the bulb. ▼

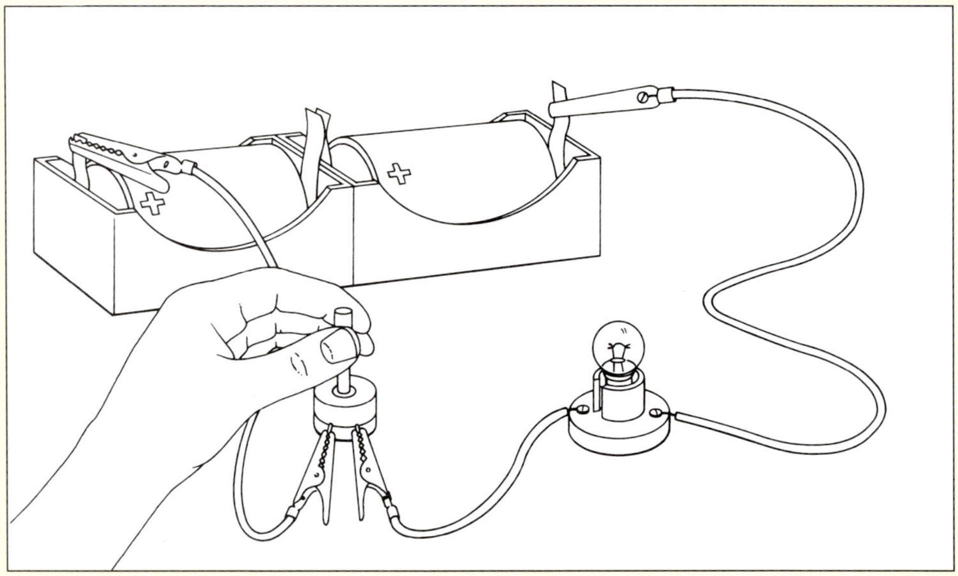

C Now build this circuit by replacing the bulb with an electric motor. ▼

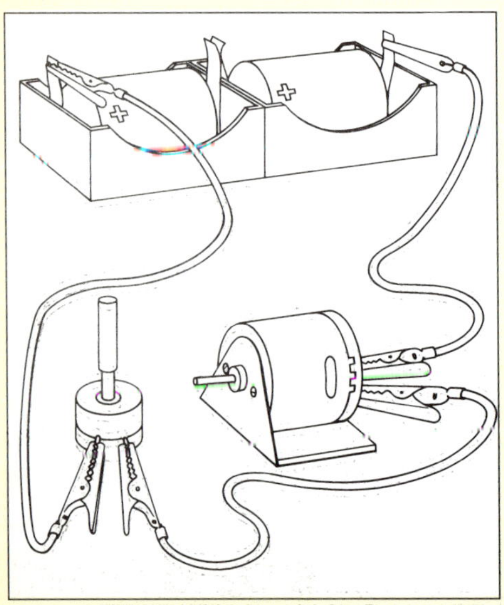

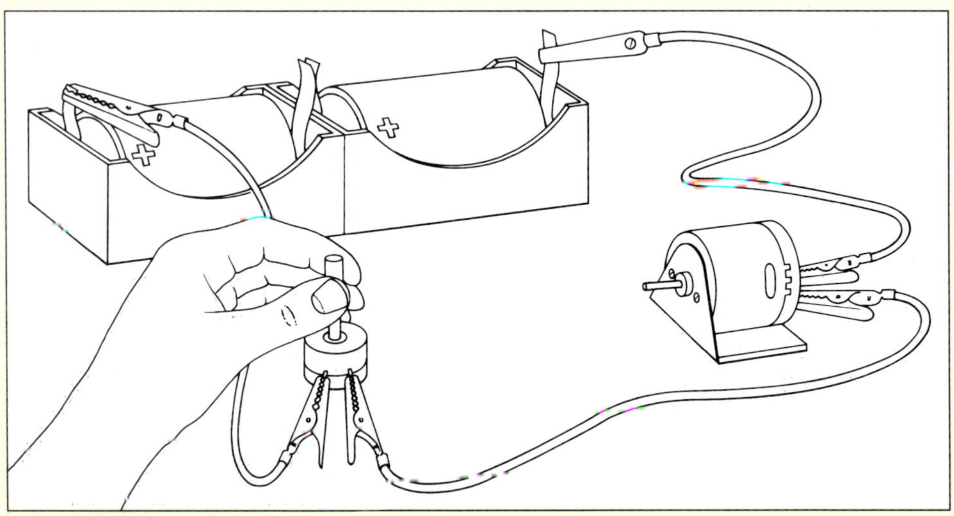

D Adjust the variable resistor and observe what happens to the motor. ▲

Q1 Write down what happens in **B** and **D** when you adjust the variable resistor.

The voltmeter connection

Let's use a **voltmeter** to measure the voltage of a battery.

Note You must connect the positive side of the voltmeter (usually the red terminal) to the positive side (+) of the battery. If you do not, the needle of the voltmeter will move the wrong way. If you are using a digital voltmeter it will show a negative (–) reading.

Q1 Copy this table.

Number of batteries	*Voltmeter reading (volts)*

Apparatus

- ☐ 2 × 1.5 V batteries
- ☐ 2 battery holders
- ☐ 2 connecting wires
- ☐ 0–5 V voltmeter
- ☐ crocodile clips

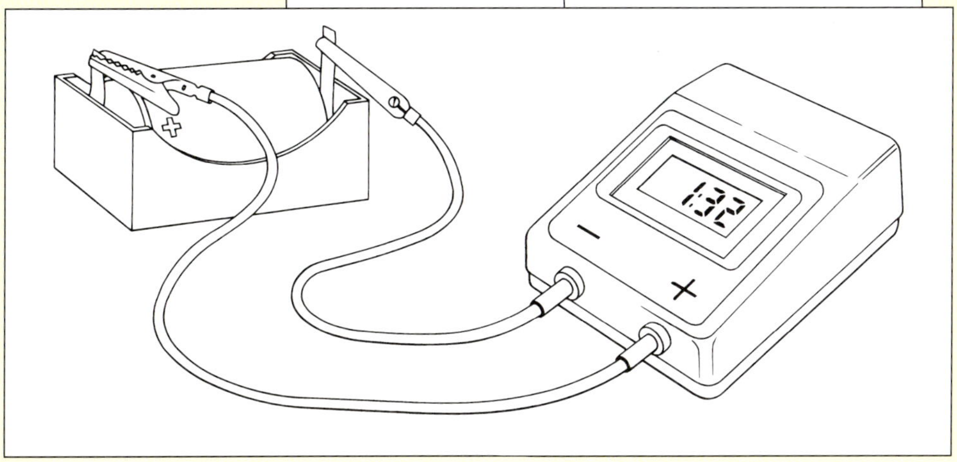

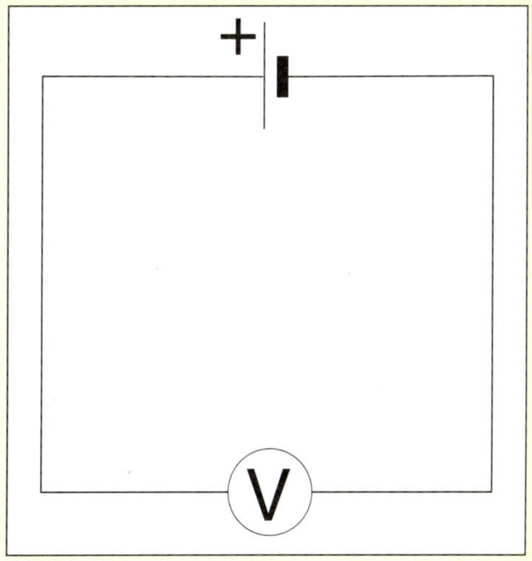

A Build this circuit. Connect a voltmeter across the battery. Read your voltmeter. Record the result in your table. ▲

B This is the circuit diagram. ▲

C Now connect a voltmeter across two batteries. Read your voltmeter. Complete the table. ▶

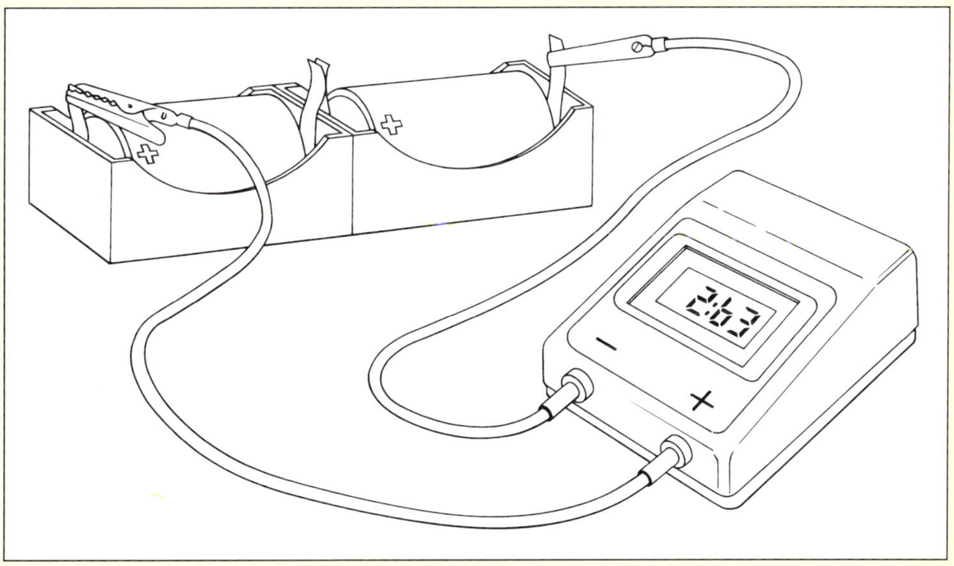

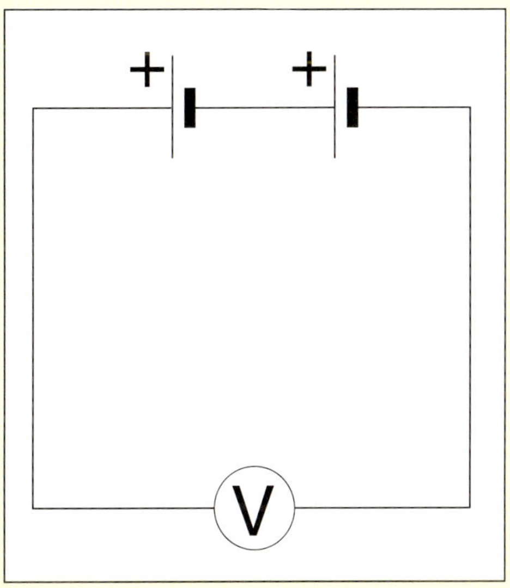

D This is the circuit diagram. Connecting two or more batteries like this, we say they are connected **in series**. ▲

Q2 What is the voltage of one battery?

Q3 Is the voltage the same as that written on the outside of the battery?

Q4 What is the voltage of two batteries connected in series?

Q5 Would you have guessed this value? Why?

Extension exercise 2 can be used now.

Measuring voltage across a circuit

The voltmeter

A voltmeter measures the number of volts across parts of an electrical circuit. A voltmeter is always connected **in parallel** across the part of the circuit to be measured.

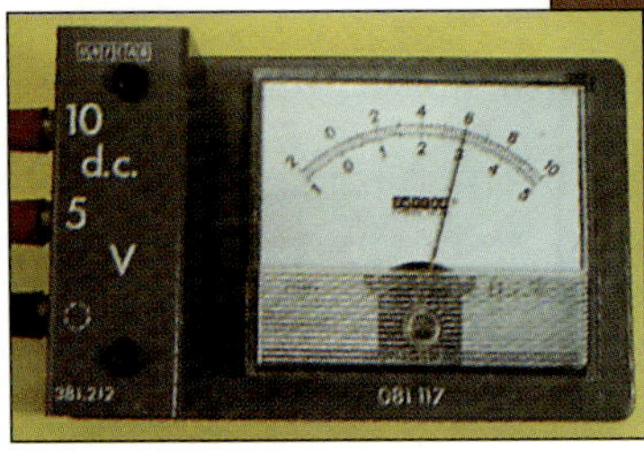

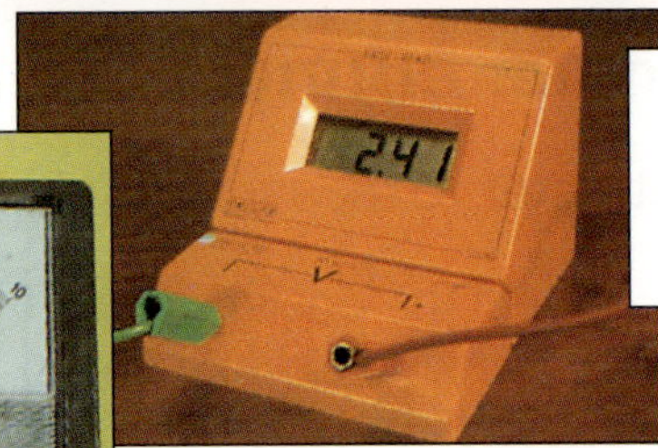

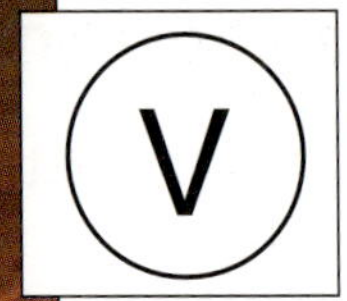

Apparatus

- ☐ 2 × 1.5 V batteries
- ☐ 2 battery holders
- ☐ 2 × 2.5 V bulbs ☐ 2 bulb holders
- ☐ small screwdriver ☐ switch
- ☐ 6 connecting wires
- ☐ 0–5 V voltmeter
- ☐ crocodile clips

In this experiment you are going to measure the number of volts across a bulb.

Q1 Copy this table.

Number of bulbs	*Voltmeter reading (volts)*

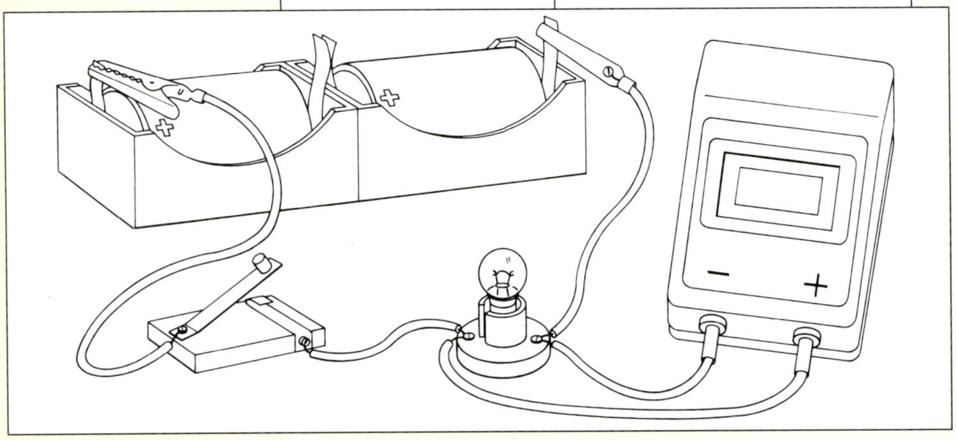

A Build this circuit. Close the switch. Read your voltmeter. Complete the table. ▲

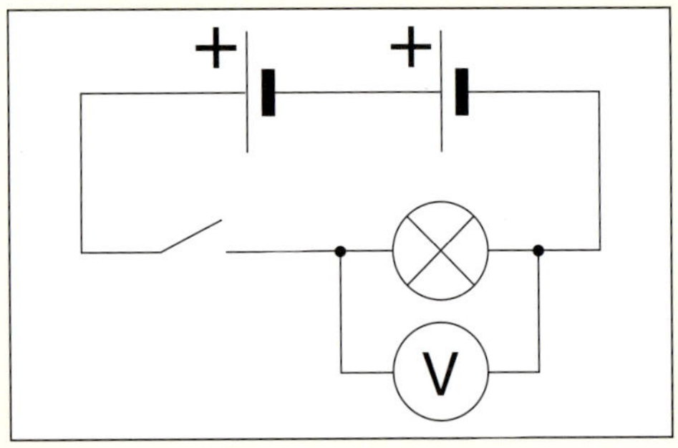

B This is the circuit diagram. The voltmeter is connected **in parallel** across the bulb. ▲

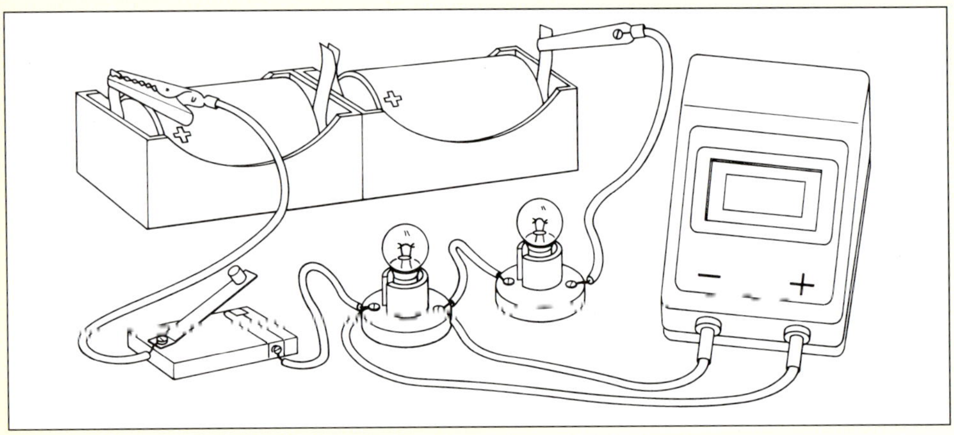

C Now build this circuit. Close the switch. Read your voltmeter. Complete the table. ▲

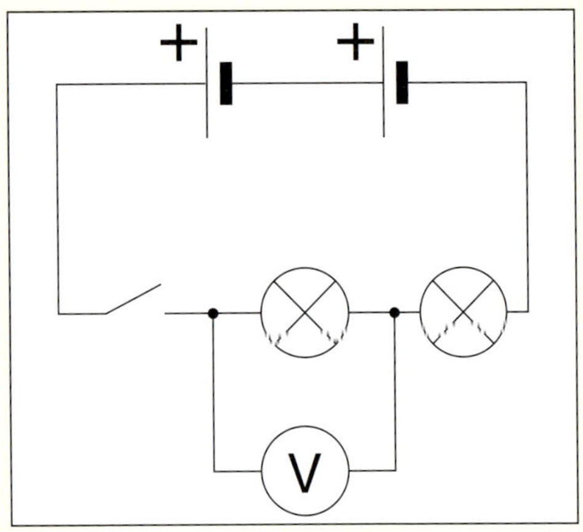

D This is the circuit diagram. ▲

Q2 What is the voltage across the bulb in **A**?

Q3 What is the voltage across the bulb in **C**?

Q4 Compare your answers to **Q2** and **Q3**. What do you notice about the results?

Extension exercise 3 can be used now.

Measuring the current flowing through a circuit

The ammeter

We measure electric current with an ammeter. The ammeter is always connected in series with the circuit. Electric current is measured in **amperes (amps)**.

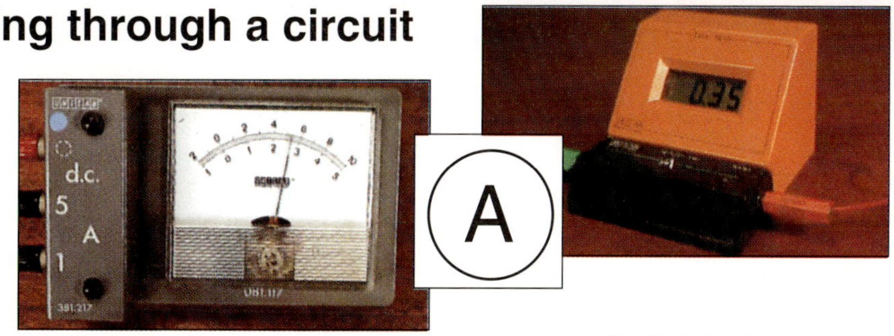

In this experiment you are going to use an **ammeter** to measure the current flowing through a circuit.

Note You must connect the ammeter correctly. If you don't the needle of the ammeter will move the wrong way. If you are using a digital ammeter you will get a negative (–) reading.

Q1 Copy this table.

Position of ammeter	*Ammeter reading (amps)*
between the battery and the lamp	

Apparatus

- ☐ 2 × 1.5 V batteries ☐ switch
- ☐ 2 battery holders ☐ 2.5 V bulb
- ☐ bulb holder ☐ 0–1 A ammeter
- ☐ small screwdriver
- ☐ 4 connecting wires
- ☐ crocodile clips

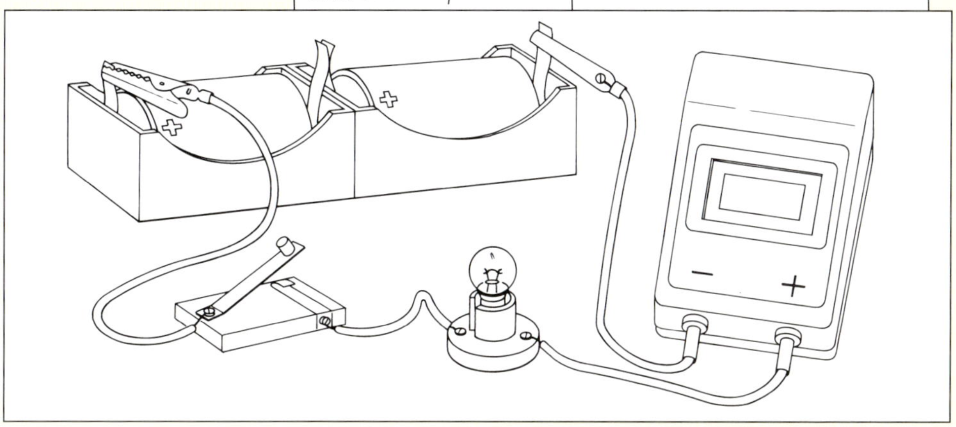

A Build this circuit. Close the switch. Read the ammeter. Complete the table. ▲

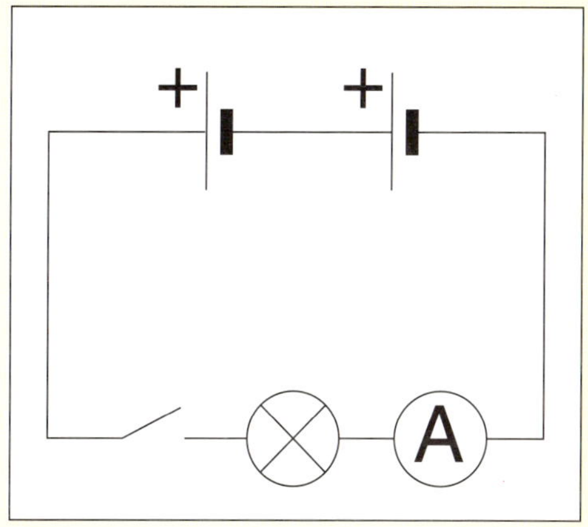

B This is the circuit diagram. ▲

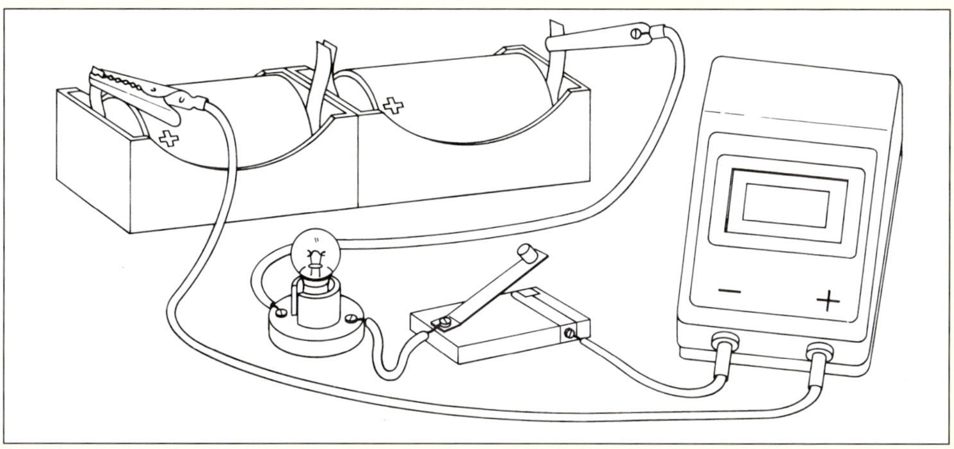

C Now build this circuit. ▲
Note The ammeter is in a different position. Close the switch. Read the ammeter. Complete the table.

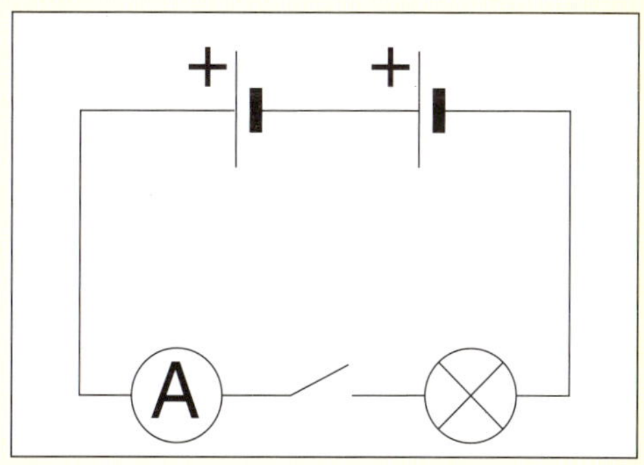

D This is the circuit diagram. ▲

Q2 Does the position of the ammeter affect the reading?

Extension exercise 4 can be used now.

3 Resistance

What is resistance?

Resistance

The wire you will use in the experiment resists and reduces the flow of current through the circuit. It is called resistance wire. Some materials like **constantan** and **nichrome** have a high resistance, others like copper have a low resistance.

In this experiment you are going to use an ammeter and a voltmeter to find the **resistance** of a piece of wire.

Apparatus

- ☐ low voltage d.c. power supply
- ☐ 0–1 A ammeter
- ☐ 0–5 V voltmeter
- ☐ 0–25 ohm variable resistor
- ☐ switch
- ☐ metre length of 34 s.w.g. constantan wire
- ☐ 6 connecting wires
- ☐ 6.5 V 0.3 A bulb with holder
- ☐ crocodile clips

Q1 Copy this table.

Voltage (volts)	Current (amps)	Resistance (ohms) $= \frac{\text{Voltage}}{\text{Current}}$

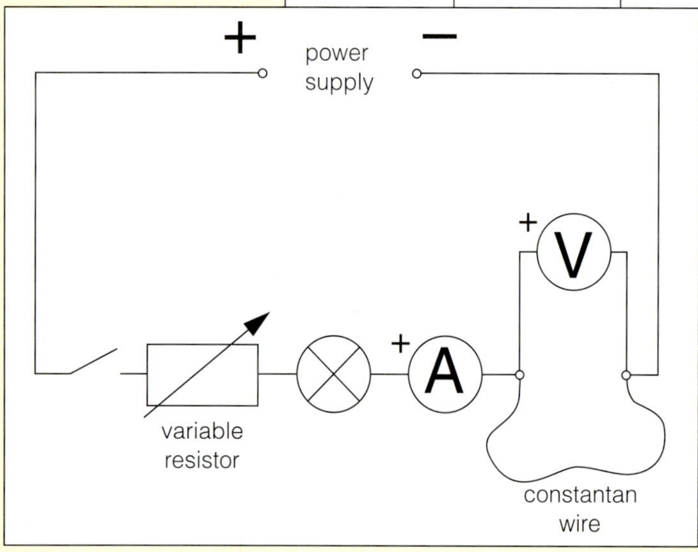

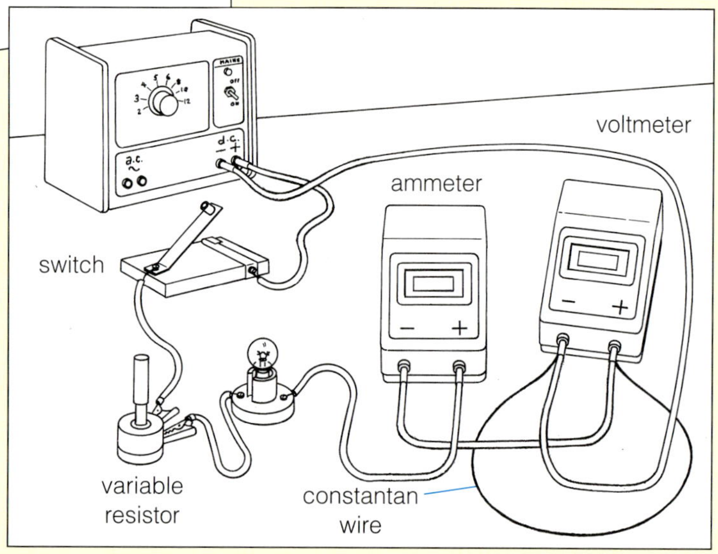

A Build this circuit. Ask your teacher to check your circuit. ▲

B Set the power supply unit to 6 V. Switch it on. Close the circuit switch. ▲

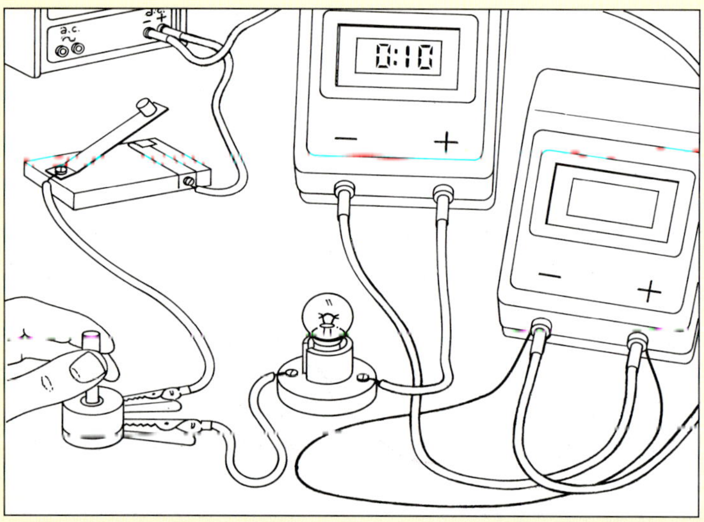

C Adjust the variable resistor to set the ammeter reading to 0.1 A. Record this value and the voltmeter reading in your table. ◀

D Repeat **C** four more times. Adjust the variable resistor to change the value of the current. Record the new value for current and voltage in your table.

Q2 Complete column 3 in your table.

Q3 What do you notice about the results in the resistance column?

Extension exercise 5 can be used now.

Series and parallel

Bulbs can be connected together in series or in parallel.

Q1 Copy this table.

I predict the ______ circuit will be brighter		
Number of bulbs	Series or parallel	Brightness of bulbs
1	series	
2		

Apparatus

- ☐ 2 x 1.5V batteries
- ☐ 2 battery holders
- ☐ 2 x 2.5V bulbs
- ☐ 2 bulb holders
- ☐ crocodile clips
- ☐ connecting wires

Q2 Predict which arrangement of bulbs will give most light. Give a reason.

Series

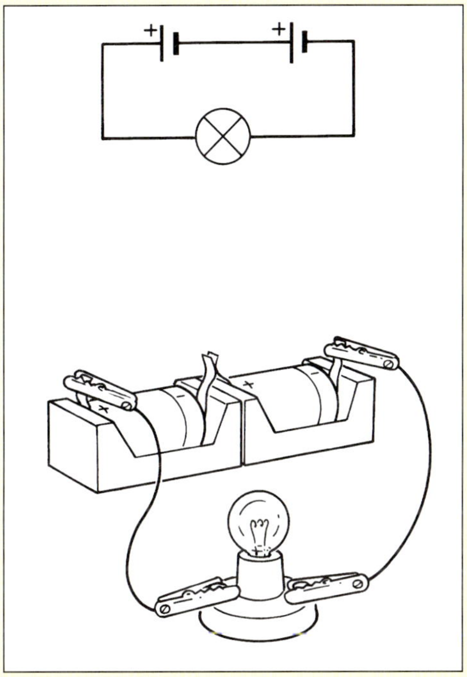

A Build this circuit. Complete the table. ▲

B Alter **A** by putting another bulb in series. Complete the table. ▲

Parallel

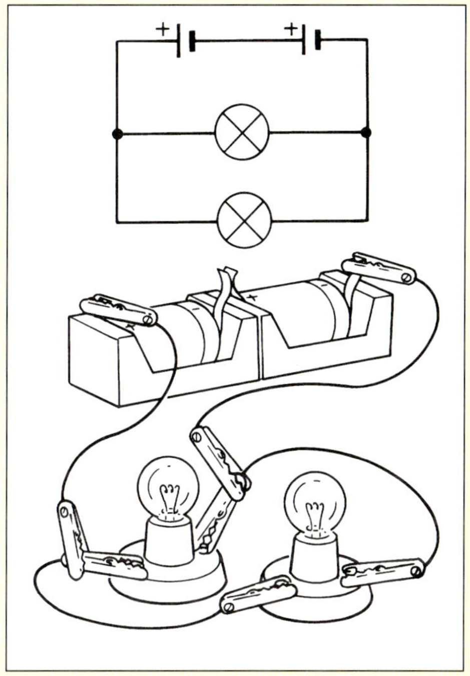

C Build this circuit. Complete the table. ▲

D Alter circuit **C** by putting another bulb in parallel. Complete the table.

When you add a second bulb in series its resistance is added to the total. More resistance in the circuit means a smaller current flowing. The bulbs get dimmer.

Q3 What happens when you unscrew one of the bulbs in circuit B?

Q4 Write down what happens when you unscrew one of the bulbs in circuit **C**? How is this different to circuit **B**?

Q5 Which circuit transfers most energy from the batteries?

Q6 Was your prediction about the brightness of the bulbs correct? How can you improve the experiment by measuring the current flowing through each bulb?

Extension exercise 6 can be used now.

Diodes: a one-way street

A diode is a device which has a high resistance in one direction and a low resistance in the other. Current will flow one way but not the other.

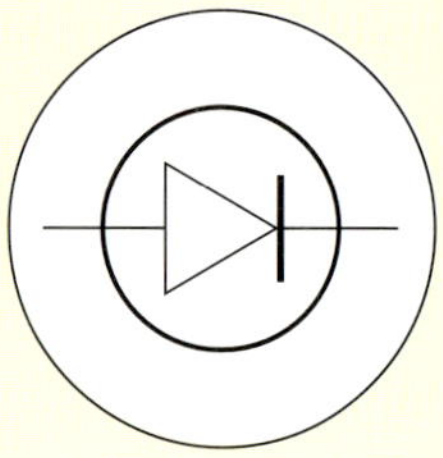

Apparatus

- ☐ 1.5 V battery ☐ battery holder
- ☐ diode ☐ 1.5 V bulb
- ☐ bulb holder ☐ ammeter
- ☐ voltmeter ☐ variable resistor
- ☐ connecting wires
- ☐ crocodile clips

Direction of diode	*Lamp on/off*
facing in one direction	
facing in the opposite direction	

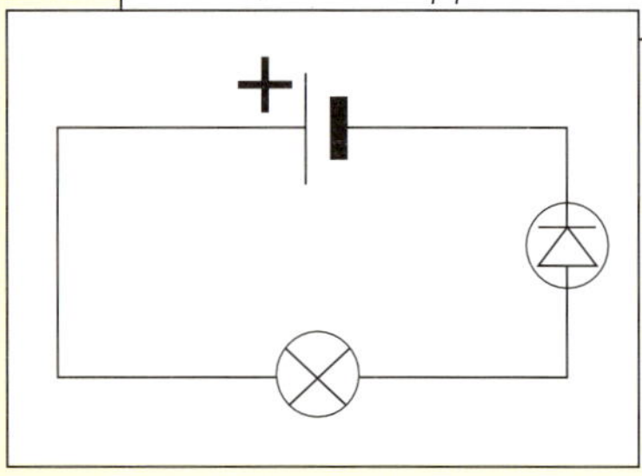

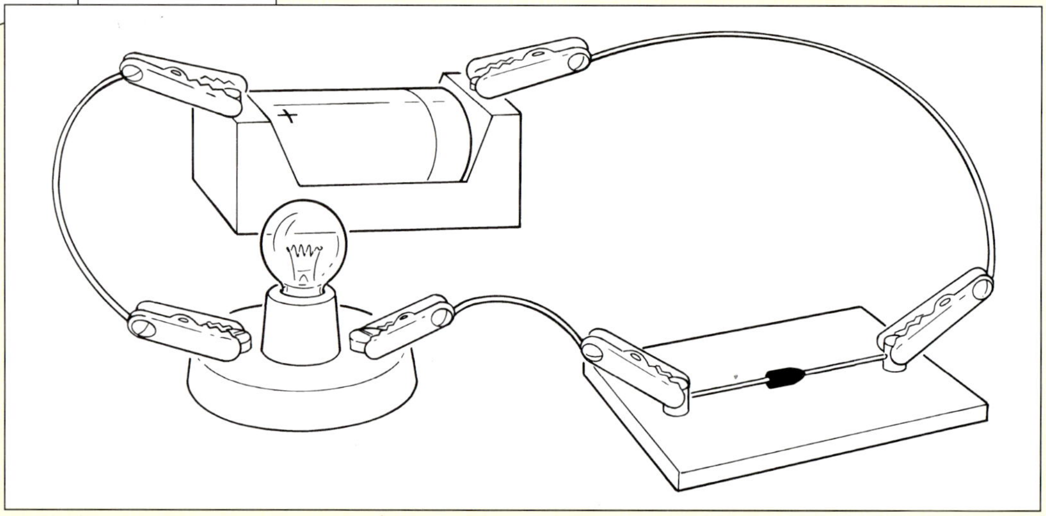

A Connect up the circuit. Complete the table. ▲

B Turn the diode round in the circuit. Complete the table. ▶

Q1 How does the bulb help you to find out what the diode is doing?

Q2 Copy this table.

Voltage (volts)	*Current (amps)*	*Resistance (ohms)* = *voltage / current*

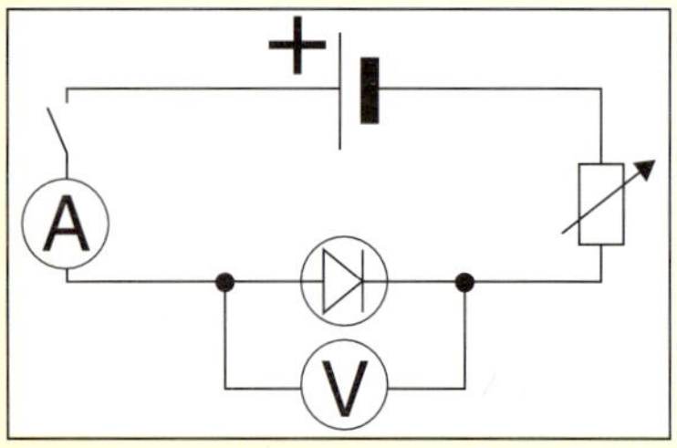

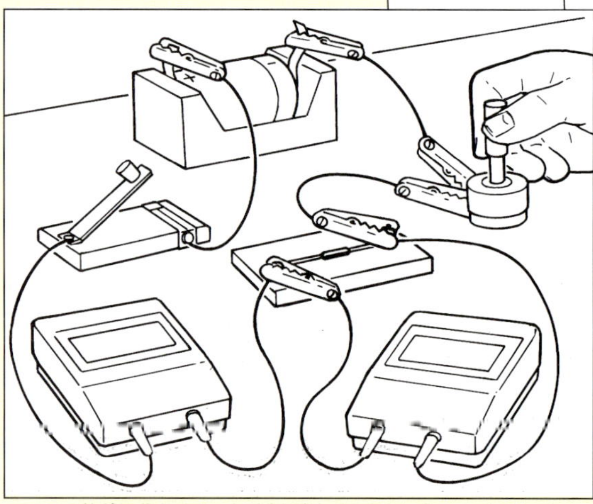

C Build this circuit. Check that the diode conducts. ▲

D Set the power supply to 6V. Switch it on and close the circuit switch. ▶

Q3 Plot a graph of voltage against current from the results in your table. The axes should look like this.

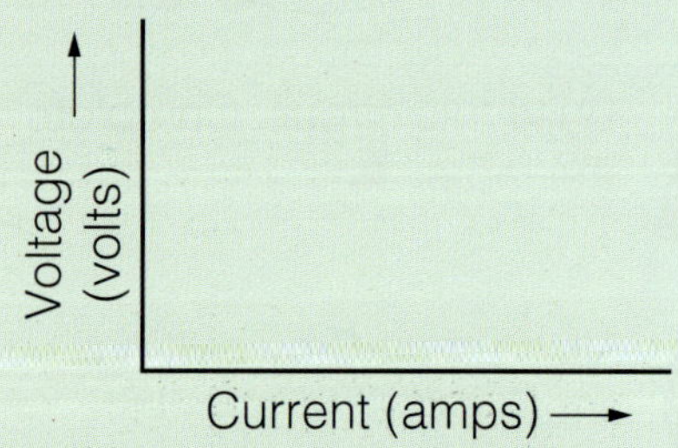

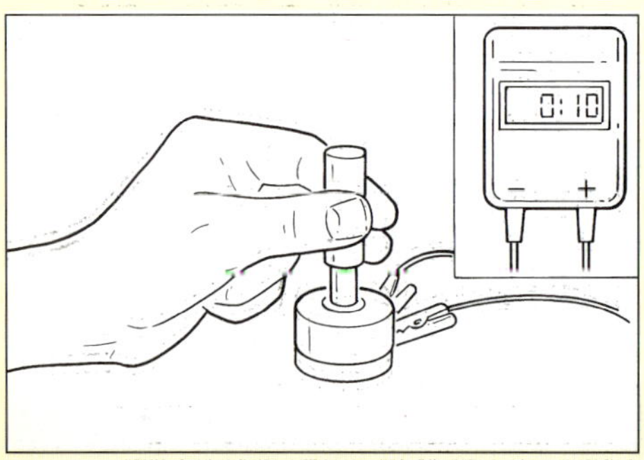

E Adjust the variable resistor to get the ammeter reading to 0.1A. Record the current and voltmeter reading in the table. ◀

F Repeat **E** four more times, adjusting the variable resistor to change the current. Record the new values for current and voltage in the table.

Q4 What happens to the current as the voltage increases?

Q5 The amplifier in a personal stereo will be damaged if the batteries are put in the wrong way round. What would you use to protect the amplifier from damage? Where would you put the device?

Light sensors

▶ The light sensor contains a special cell which is sensitive to light. This device is very fragile and is covered with plastic for protection. The plastic is clear at the front to let light in. On the opposite side a coloured layer stops light entering from the back. The light sensor does not have any moving parts. Electrical connections are made to the two wires.

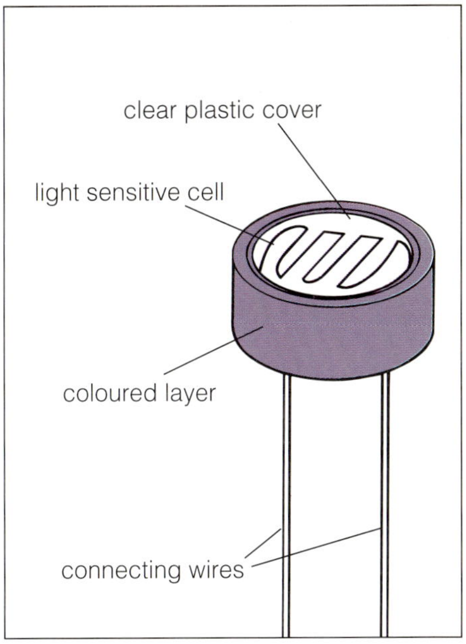

▼ When a bright light shines on the sensor, the resistance of the cell decreases. The cell lets electric current flow through it. We say it is switched 'on'.
In darkness the resistance of the cell increases. The cell will not let as much electric current flow. We say that the cell is switched 'off'.

You can compare the flow of electric current to the flow of water from a tap. The tap can be adjusted to give any flow of water between fully on and completely off.

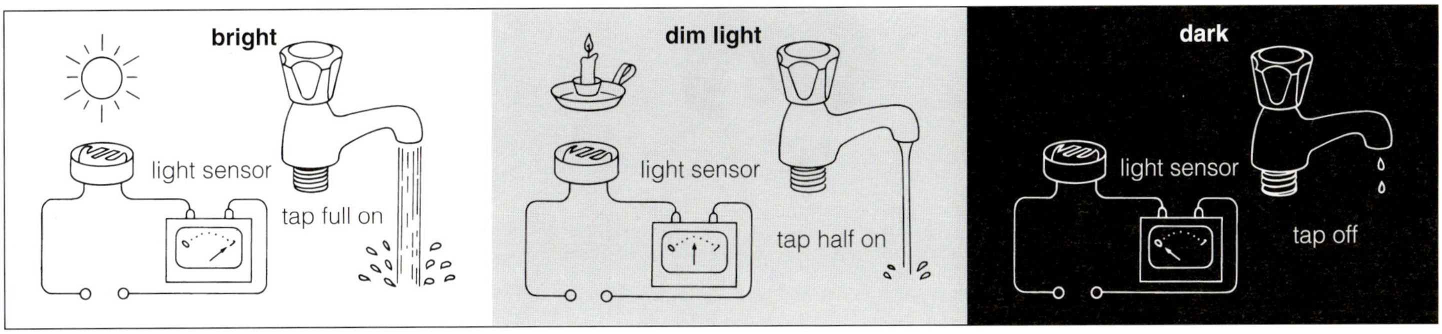

◀ Most modern cameras have 'fully automatic **exposure control**'. This means the camera will take correctly exposed photographs in bright or dull light.

A light sensor is electrically connected to the camera **shutter**. When a photograph is taken on a sunny day the light control system operates the shutter so that only a small amount of bright light reaches the film to expose it correctly.

On a dull day the light sensor keeps the shutter open for a longer time so that once again the film is correctly exposed.

Q1 Why does the light sensor have a high resistance?

4 Heating by an electric current

The heating effect

When electricity flows there is a heating effect. Most times it is very small but it is always there. The heating effect is used in a lot of things such as kettles and fires.

Let us find out how electricity flowing in a bulb affects how hot it gets.

Q1 Copy this table.

Voltage (V)	Current (A)	Temperature (°C)
6		
8		
10		

A Build this circuit. ▼

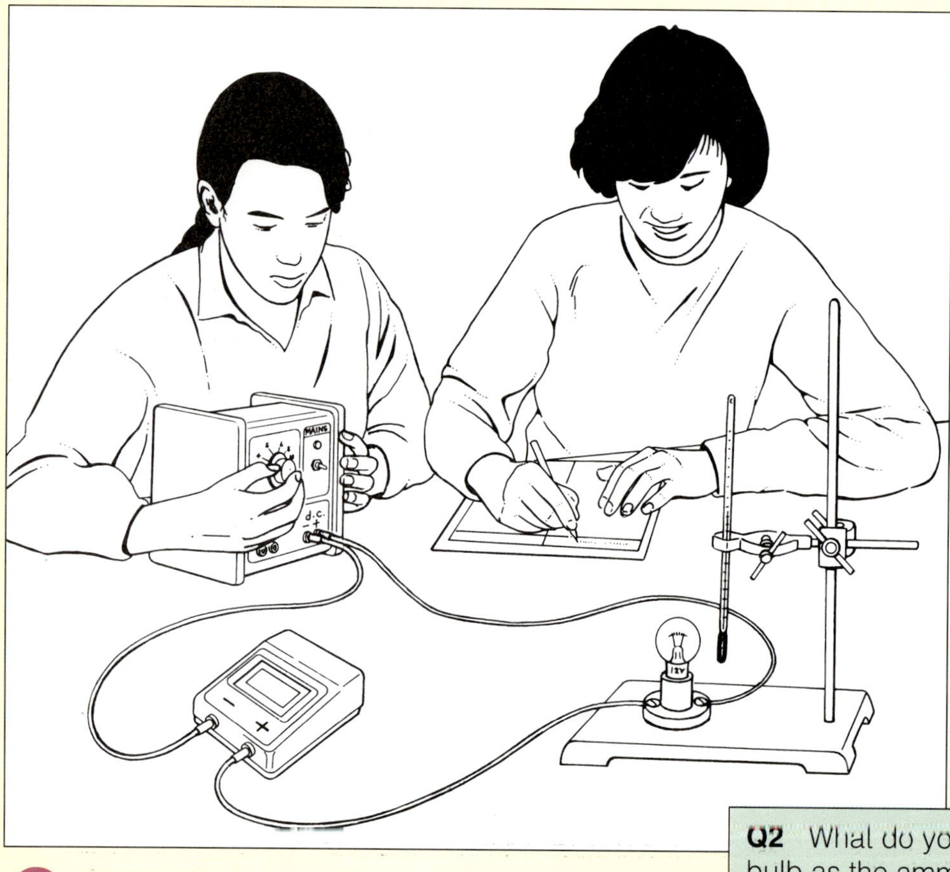

Apparatus

- ☐ low voltage power supply
- ☐ 12 V 5 W car bulb and holder
- ☐ stop watch ☐ 0–1 A ammeter
- ☐ thermometer and holder

Safety Warning
Avoid burning your fingers.

B Put the thermometer 1 cm from the car bulb so that it is easy to see the scale. Read the thermometer and fill in the start temperature in the table. ▼

C Set the power supply to 6 volts. Switch on and wait for one minute. Read the thermometer and the ammeter and look carefully at the bulb. Fill in the second line of the table. ▲

D Increase the setting on the power supply to the next highest. Wait one minute, take the readings and fill in the table. Repeat **D** until the setting on the power supply is 10 volts.

Q2 What do you notice about the brightness of the bulb as the ammeter reading gets higher?

Q3 What happens to the temperature as the bulb gets brighter?

Q4 What colour changes happen as the bulb gets hotter?

Q5 What might happen if the bulb got very bright?

Extension exercise 7 can be used now.

Keeping us warm

We use the heating effect of a current to keep us warm.

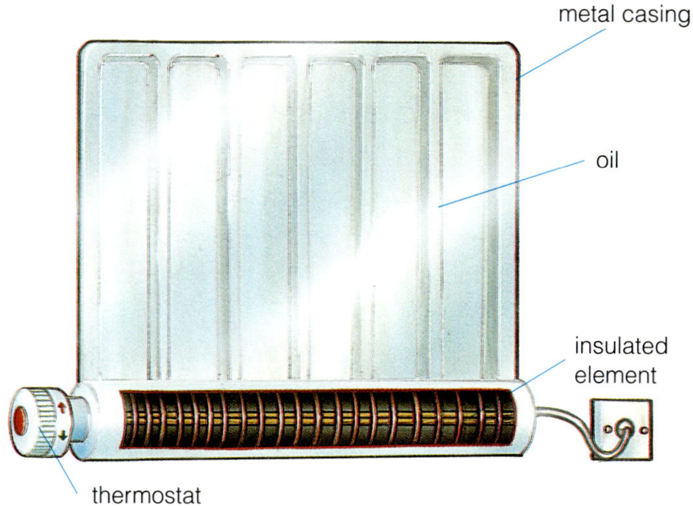

▲ The heater is filled with oil that is warmed by an electrical heating element inside it. The air round the heater gets warm and rises. This type of heater is useful for giving background heat.

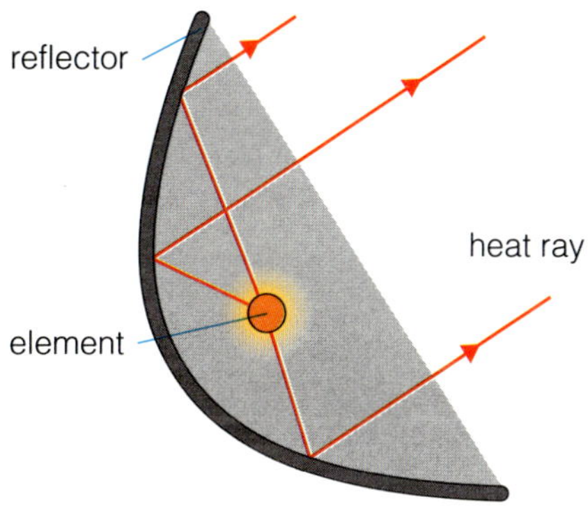

▲ This heater has an electrical element that glows red hot. The heat from this fire is infra-red waves. There is a mirror behind the element and this reflects the heat forwards. The heater is used where a quick source of heat is needed for a short time.

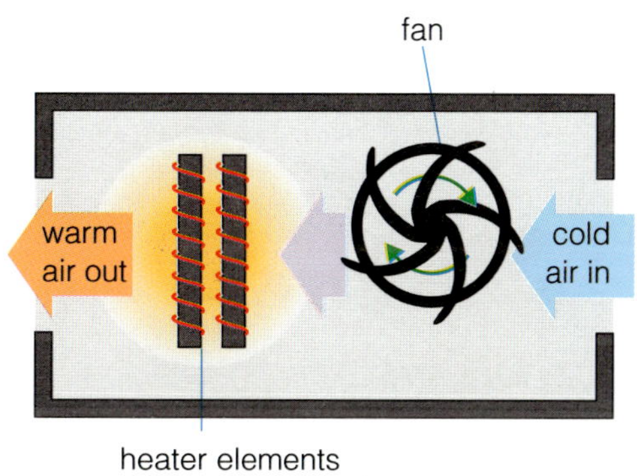

▲ There is a fan behind the heating element in this heater to blow warm air forwards. A second heating element can be switched on to give a greater heat output.

Q1 For each heater write down how the heat is produced and where the heat goes to.

Q2 Which heater would be very dangerous for small children?

Q3 A hairdrier is similar to one of these heaters. Which is it similar to and why?

Q4 Which of these heaters could still be useful on a summer day?

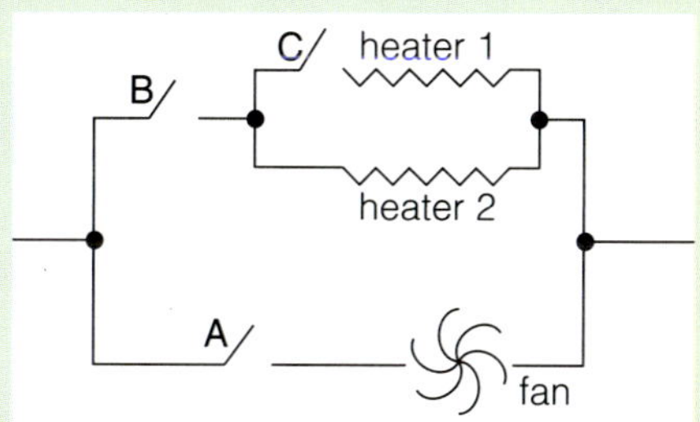

Q5 What would be the effect of
a closing switches A, B and C?
b closing switches A and B?
c closing switch A only?

Q6 Why should switches B or C never be closed without closing A?

Q7 How could you improve this circuit so that this never happens?

Cookers

▶ Modern cookers use many different ways to heat food. Ovens have heating elements to warm the air and many ovens have fans installed that blow the hot air. Grills use electrical elements that glow red hot to heat the food. The energy is carried as infra-red waves.

The hob is used for heating pans of food. Some hobs have elements that heat the base of the pan directly. The base of the pan must be flat so that the heat conducts into the pan quickly. Radiant hobs glow with a red light. The heat comes from infra-red waves and the hob warms up and cools down very quickly.

Some modern cookers have a ceramic top made from a special glass. The heating areas are marked on the surface. The glass warms up quickly where the heating areas are but stays cool elsewhere.

There are some hobs that stay completely cool. They use magnetism to warm the metal in the base of a pan placed on the hob. This type of hob wastes very little energy because nothing else gets hot.

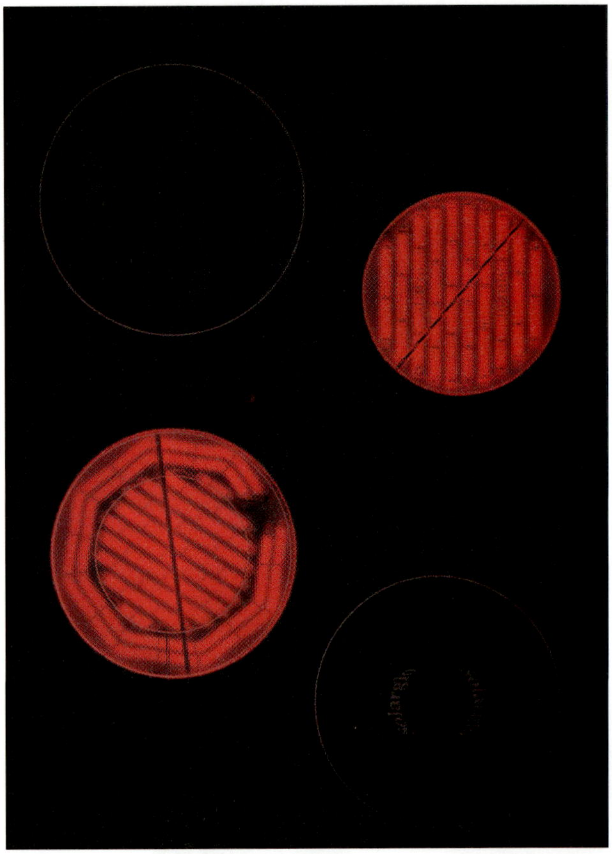

◀ When you heat something up its molecules vibrate faster. Microwaves are electromagnetic waves. They get right inside the food. The energy of the waves is absorbed by any water in the food. The water molecules start to vibrate more strongly, then the food gets hot and cooks very quickly.

▶ A slow cooker is an insulated box with a small electrical heating element to cook the food. The current flowing through the heater is small so it takes a long time for the food to cook. However, it is very cheap to run.

Q1 Make a list of the different kinds of electric cookers available. See if you can find any other types than those listed on this page. What are the advantages of each type of cooker?

Q2 You are asked by a consumer group to compare the efficiency of a grill and a microwave cooker. Design (on paper) a fair test to decide which is best.

Saving energy

In our homes and at work we all use large amounts of electrical energy. We need to save as much energy as we can.

▶ Electrical equipment is now being made that uses less electricity. This washing machine can use less water so it needs less electricity to heat it. Washing powders can work at lower temperatures so the water used does not need to be as hot.

▼ Electrical heaters have a thermostat to switch them off when they reach the right temperature. This saves energy by not allowing rooms to get too hot.

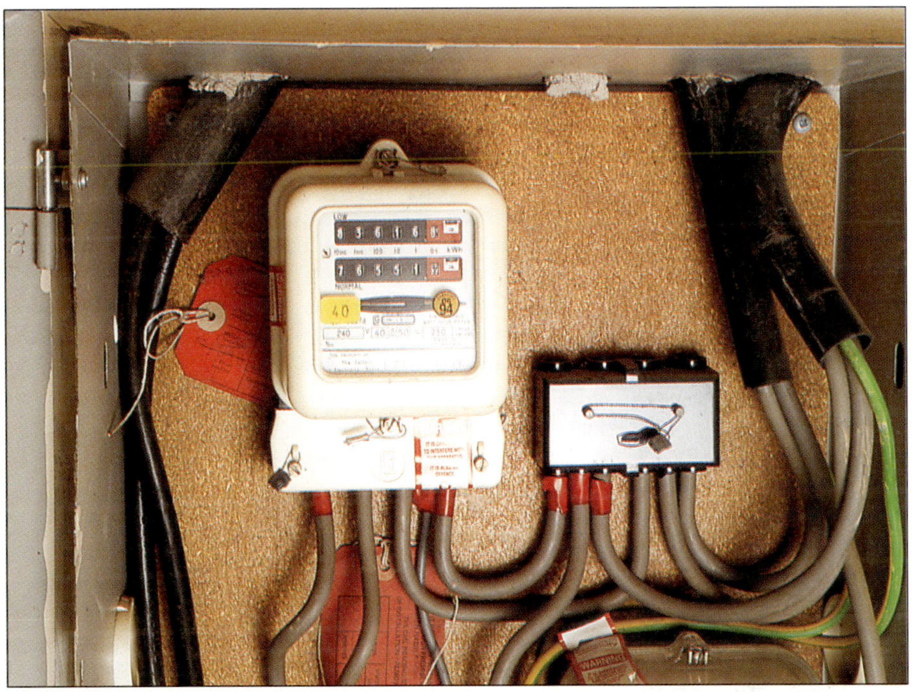

◀ We cannot store electricity. The power stations must run all night. The electricity company sells cheap electricity at night. This is a special white meter. It measures how much cheap electricity is used by storage radiators.

Q1 Write down three heating devices that are fitted with a thermostat to control their temperatures.

Q2 Why is it important for all of us to use less electricity?

Q3 Your school wants to save money by switching off lights in empty rooms. Make a poster to remind people to switch off when leaving a room.

Extension exercise 8 can be used now.

How hot does it get?

Let us look at how water's temperature changes when we heat it up. Does the size of the electric current affect the temperature?

Apparatus

- ☐ ammeter
- ☐ immersion heater
- ☐ beaker
- ☐ measuring cylinder
- ☐ power supply
- ☐ thermometer
- ☐ connecting wires

Safety Warning
Caution, the immersion heater will get very hot. Do not allow them to cool immersed in water.

Q1 Predict what will happen if we double the current. Give a reason for your prediction.

Q2 Copy the table.

Time (min)	1	2	3	4	5	6	7	8	9	10	11	12	13	14	15
Temperature (°C)															

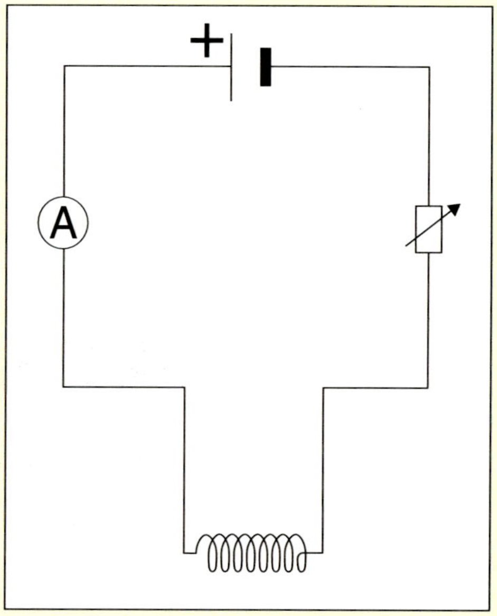

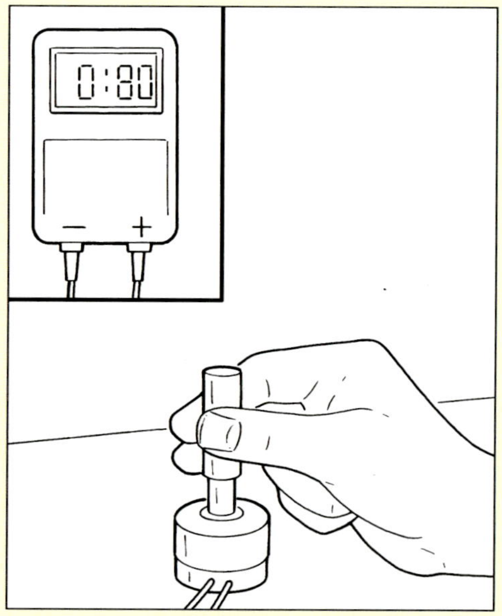

A Measure 150 cm^3 of water in the measuring cylinder. Pour the water into the beaker. ▲

B Set up the circuit. Place the immersion heater in the beaker. ▲

C Set the variable resistor so that the ammeter reads 0.8 A. ▲

D Take the temperature of the water at the start. Switch on and take the temperature each minute for 15 minutes. Complete the table. ▶

E Make a new copy of the table. Set the variable resistor to give an ammeter reading of 1.6 A.

F Repeat **A** to **D**.

Q3 Draw a graph with two sets of results on one set of axes.

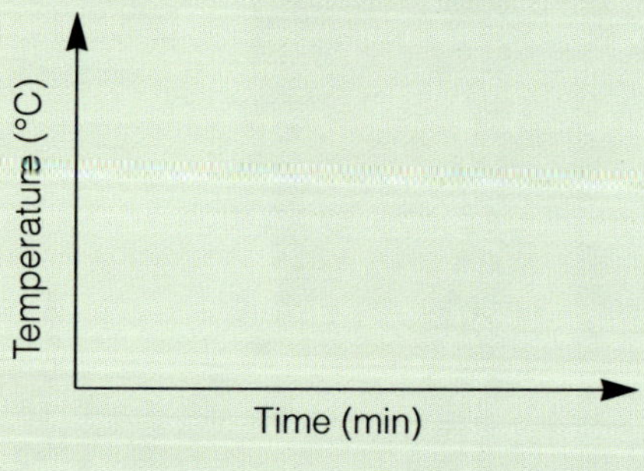

Q4 Was your prediction correct?

Q5 How could you improve your experiment?

5 Electrical safety

Fuses and circuit breakers

The main **fuses** in a house are near the electricity meter. They protect the house wiring from overheating if too much electricity flows or because of a fault. A house usually has separate fuses for sockets and for lights and a special fuse for a cooker. Modern houses and factories have **circuit breakers** in place of fuses. They detect when too large a current is flowing and switch the circuit off. They can be reset when the fault has been put right.

A special circuit breaker called a residual current circuit breaker (RCCB) detects when the current flowing into the circuit is different from that flowing out. This happens when electricity is leaking away. It is dangerous because the user could get an electric shock from the leakage. RCCBs are used for lawn mowers and electric drills.

A fuse is a piece of special wire that melts easily when a fault occurs and too much current flows. It cuts off the electricity before it can damage things. The fault must be found and corrected. All power to the fuse box should be cut off before the fuse is replaced: not an easy thing to do if the fuse is for the lights!

Safety and danger – an overheating effect
In this experiment you are going to see how a fuse can protect a light bulb.

A Build the circuit. Set the power supply to 4 volts and switch on. ▼

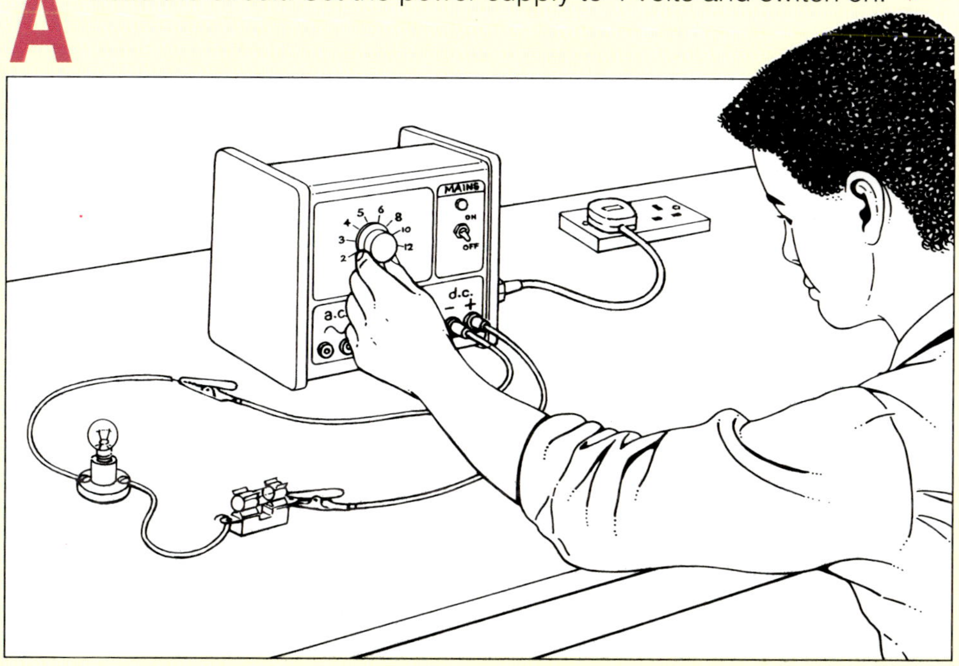

Apparatus

- ☐ low voltage d.c. power supply
- ☐ 6V 5W bulb and holder
- ☐ connecting wires
- ☐ crocodile clips
- ☐ 500 mA fuses *or* fuse wire
- ☐ fuse holder

B Increase the setting on the power supply slowly, one step at a time. When the light goes out check to see if the fuse has 'blown', that is, melted or broken.
A fuse protects equipment and wires from overheating if a fault occurs. The correct fuse should always be used.

Q1 If a fuse 'blows' in your house, why should you check what the fault is *before* replacing the fuse?

Plugs and fuses

▶ Plugs must be wired correctly to keep us safe.

> **Safety Warning**
> Altering the connections on a plug is very dangerous. Do not put the plug that you wire here into a socket.

You should always check that:

- the correct wire is connected to each terminal (look at the colours of the wires)
- no bare wire is showing where the terminal is
- the flex is not damaged and that there are no cut or worn parts
- the cord grip is holding the outer cover of the wire securely
- the plug is not cracked or damaged
- everything is tightly fastened.

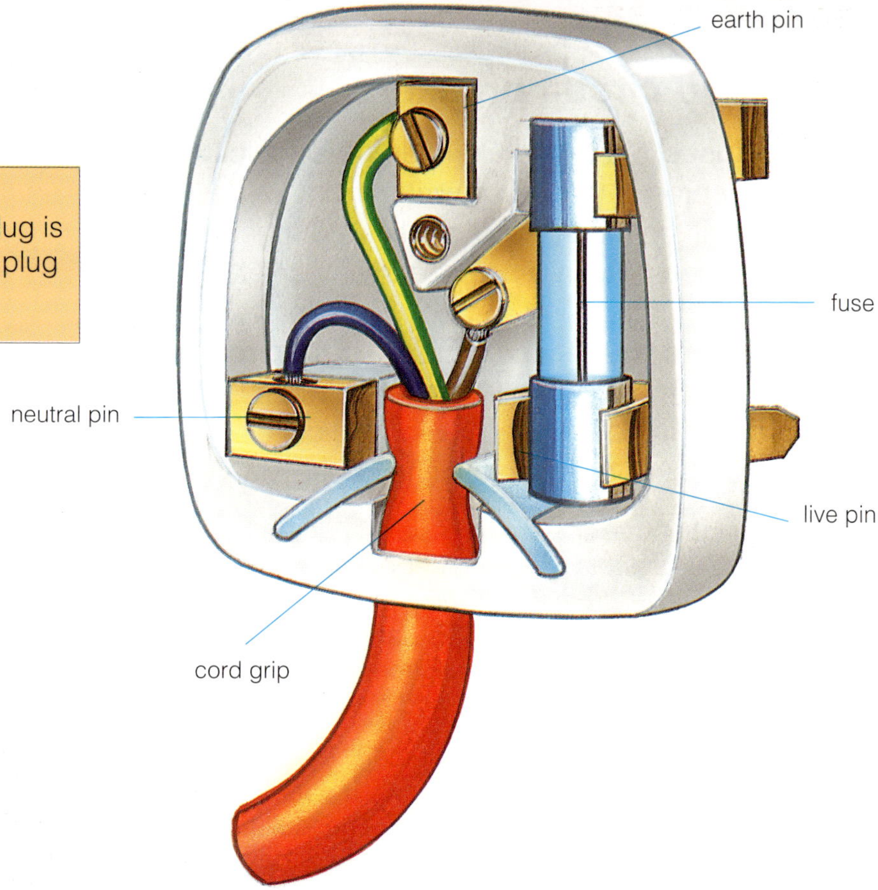

◀ The fuse in the plug protects the equipment from being damaged. The fuse is marked with the safe current that it can carry. The equipment must use a lower current than the fuse value.

Q1 Copy the table and decide on whether to fit a 3A or a 13A fuse in the plug.

Equipment	Current (A)	Fuse size
microwave	4.5	
TV	0.35	
tumble drier	9.0	
table lamp	0.25	
computer	0.9	
kettle	8.0	
hairdrier	3.5	

Q2 Which equipment in the table involves heating?

Q3 What size of fuse do all the heaters use?

Extension exercise 9 can be used now.

Keeping us safe

All these appliances have a metal case around them. The wires inside could work free and touch the case. This would make the equipment dangerous because if you touched it you would get an electric shock. To prevent this, the case is connected to the earth wire (green/yellow). This wire gives an easy pathway for electricity. If a wire touches the case, a large current flows and the fuse melts.

> **Safety Warning**
> All metal cased mains equipment must have an earth wire.

▼ These all have plastic cases. There is no danger from touching them because the cases are insulators. To give extra protection, equipment like this is double insulated. As well as the plastic outside, there is a second layer of insulation round the wires.

Q1 What sort of equipment has an earth wire?

Q2 Name three pieces of equipment in your home that have earth wires.

Q3 What sort of equipment is double insulated?

Q4 A metal cased fire has a loose live wire that touches the case. Write down what happens when it is switched on.

6 Magnetic effects

Finding out about magnets

▶ Magnets which are free to move point towards the north. This is how a compass works. We call the end of the magnet that points north the north pole. The end that points south is called the south pole. The two poles are places where the magnetism seems to come from.

Let's find out what magnets do.

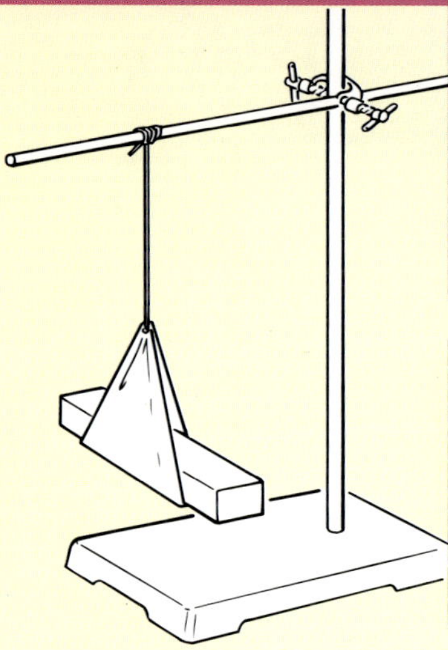

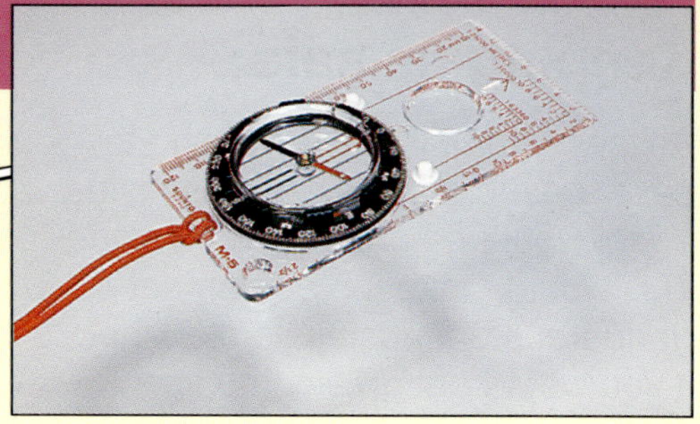

Apparatus

☐ magnet ☐ piece of paper or cloth
☐ cotton thread ☐ wooden stand
☐ bowl ☐ magnet ☐ piece of wood

A Hang the magnet up. Wait until it stops moving. Look at the direction in which the magnet is pointing. ▶

Q1 Predict what you think will happen if we float a magnet on a piece of wood in a bowl. Explain why you think this will happen.

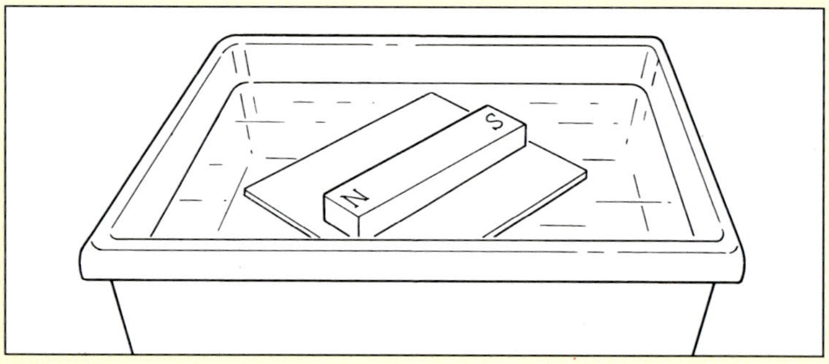

B Try the experiment. Think about whether to wait until the water stops moving before putting the wood into the bowl. ▶

Q2 What happens when the magnet is floated on the water?

Q3 What does this tell you about the size of the forces from the two poles?

Now let us look at two magnets.

C Ask your teacher how you can tell a north pole on the magnet. Push two north poles together. What can you feel? ◀

D Repeat your experiment with two south poles facing. ◀

E Try your experiment with a north pole facing a south pole. What do you feel this time? ◀

Q4 What do you feel when you push the two magnets together?

Q5 What can we say about the forces between magnets?

Magnetic patterns

We can show what the forces round magnets are like using iron filings. Iron is magnetic. The filings are pulled into patterns by the forces.

Apparatus

- ☐ iron filings and shaker ☐ card
- ☐ bar magnet

A Place a magnet under the card. Shake the iron filings gently and evenly over the card. ▶

B Tap the card lightly with a pencil to free the filings.

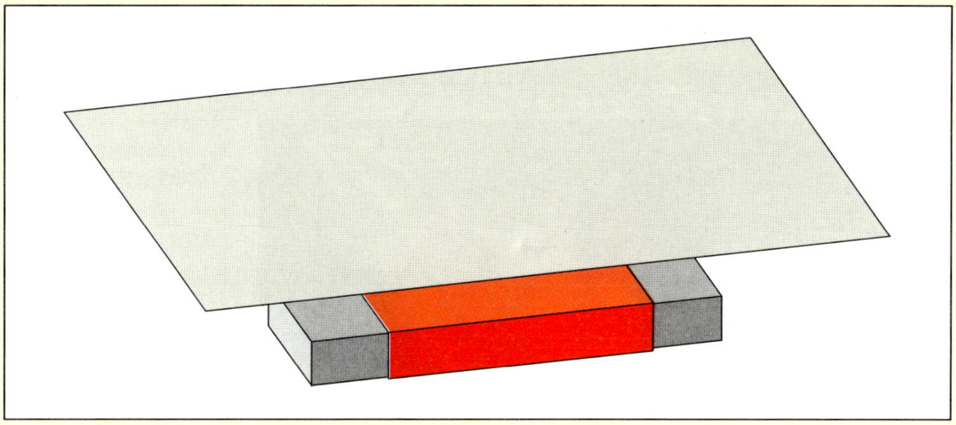

Q1 Draw the pattern the filings make in your book.

Q2 What do you notice about the patterns?

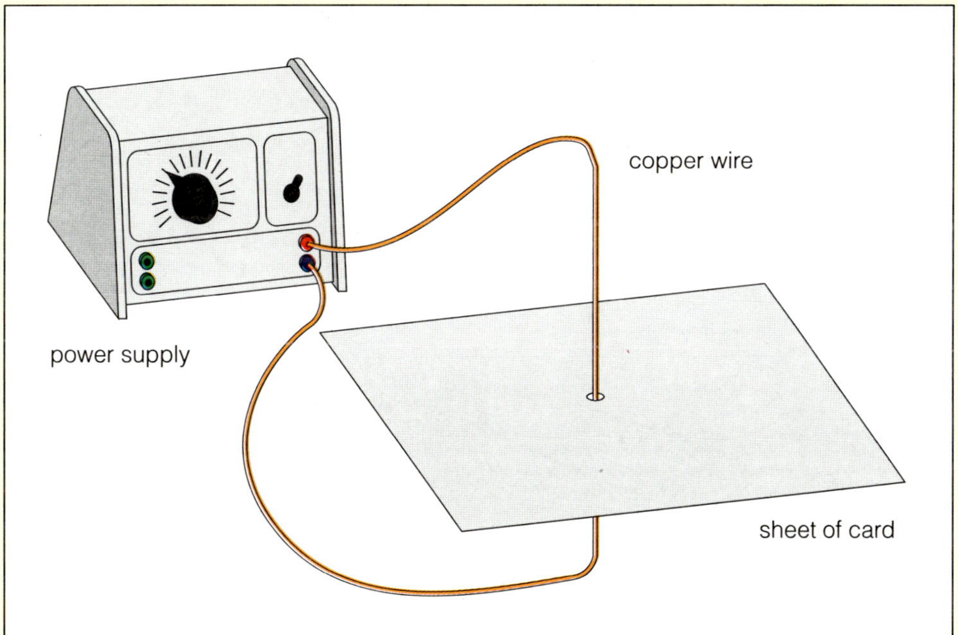

Apparatus

- ☐ power supply ☐ copper wire
- ☐ iron filings ☐ card

⚠ The copper wire will get hot because there is a big current flowing through it. Your teacher may demonstrate this experiment.

A Set up the apparatus as in the picture. ▲

B Switch on the current.

C Shake the filings onto the card and tap it with a pencil.

Q3 Sketch the pattern the filings make in your book.

Q4 What do you notice about the patterns on the card?

Q5 Is copper magnetic? (Test it with a magnet.)

Q6 Is there a magnetic force around the wire in this experiment?

Electromagnets 1

We have found that when electricity flows in a wire it behaves like a **magnet**.

We can use this effect to make **electromagnets**.

Electromagnets can **repel** (push) or **attract** (pull). They can be switched on and off. They always need electricity to make them work.

An electromagnet lifts this train off its track. It moves very smoothly. ▲

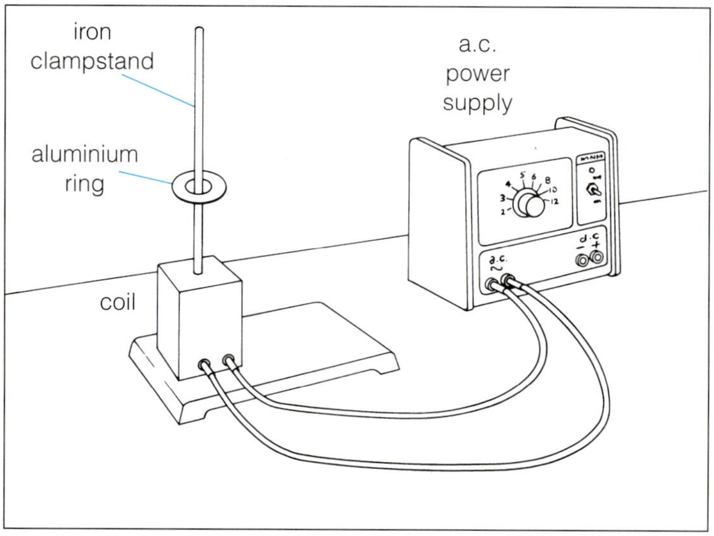

Your teacher will show you this floating effect. The ring gets warm. ▲

Electromagnets are especially useful because they can easily be turned on and off.

This very large electromagnet is being used to pick up scrap iron and drop it in a different place. ▼

This electromagnet is small but quite strong. Your teacher will show you how it works. ▼

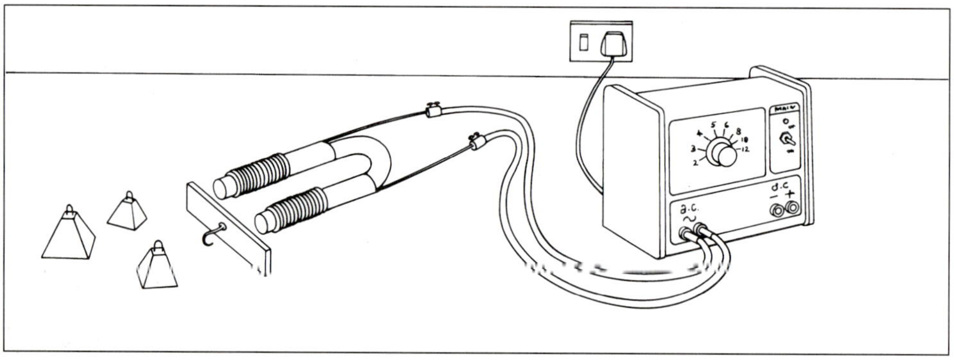

Q1 How are electromagnets like permanent magnets?

Q2 What do electromagnets need to keep them working?

Q3 What can you do with an electromagnet that you cannot do with a permanent magnet?

Q4 Why can you use an electromagnet but not a permanent magnet in the workings of an automatic shop door?

Electromagnets 2

In this experiment you are going to compare the strengths of different electromagnets.

Apparatus
☐ low voltage d.c. power supply
☐ crocodile clips ☐ iron rods
☐ paper-clips ☐ sticky tape
☐ ready-made coils ☐ cutters
☐ pencil ☐ connecting wires

A Take the coil with 30 turns of wire on it. Put the coil over the pencil and put sticky tape round to hold it. ▼

B Build this circuit. Use connecting wires and crocodile clips to connect the coil to the power supply. Set the power supply to 2V and switch on. ▼

C Put the coil into the pile of paper-clips and then raise it. How many clips are attracted? Switch off the power supply. ▼

D Take out the pencil from the coil and replace it with an iron rod. Repeat **B** and **C**. How many clips are attracted now? Switch off the power. ▼

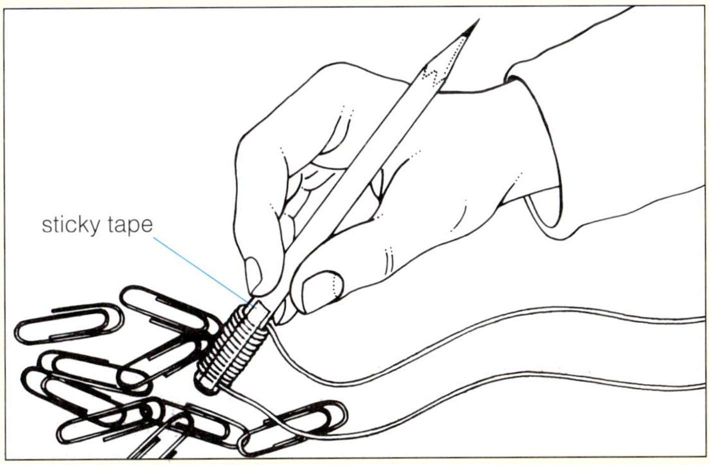

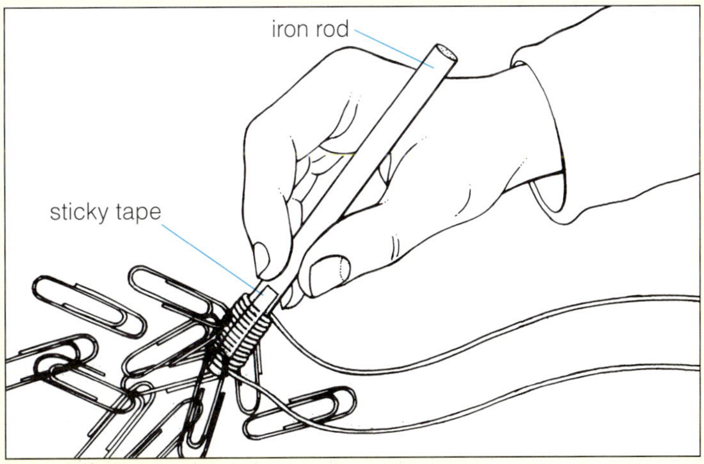

E Replace the 30 turn coil with the 70 turn coil. Switch on the power supply. How many paper-clips does the electromagnet attract now?

F Now increase the setting on the power supply to 4V. How many paper-clips does the electromagnet attract now? Switch off the power supply.

Q1 Copy and complete the following sentences. Use the correct word from each set.

The magnetic effect of a coil is best when there is a pencil/iron rod inside it, when there are a few/many turns and when there is a lot of/not much electricity flowing.

▶ An electric bell uses an electromagnet to make it work. The electromagnet attracts the spring steel clapper. The clapper hits the bell. The current for the electromagnet flows through the make-and-break and when the clapper moves the circuit is broken. This allows the clapper to spring back and the process repeats itself. The electromagnet switches itself on and off over and over again giving the ringing tone of the bell.

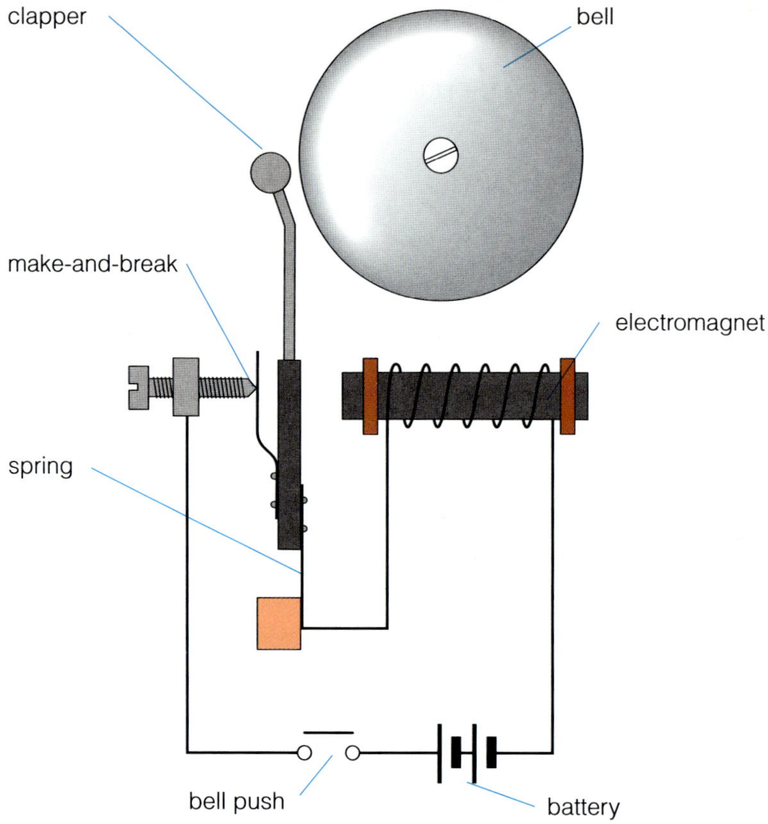

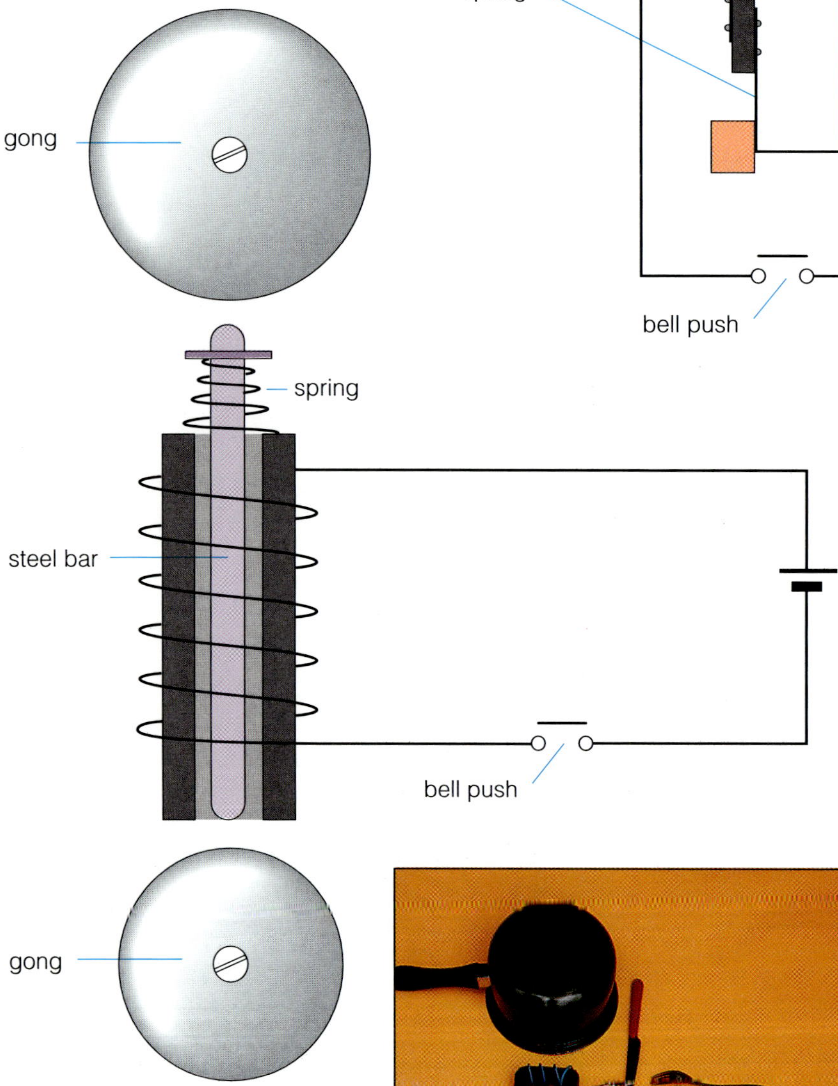

◀ A door chime does not need to keep on ringing like a bell. When the button is pressed, the steel bar is pulled through the electromagnet and hits the bottom gong. When the button is released, the spring pulls the bar back and it hits the top gong. This gives the double 'ding dong' sound.

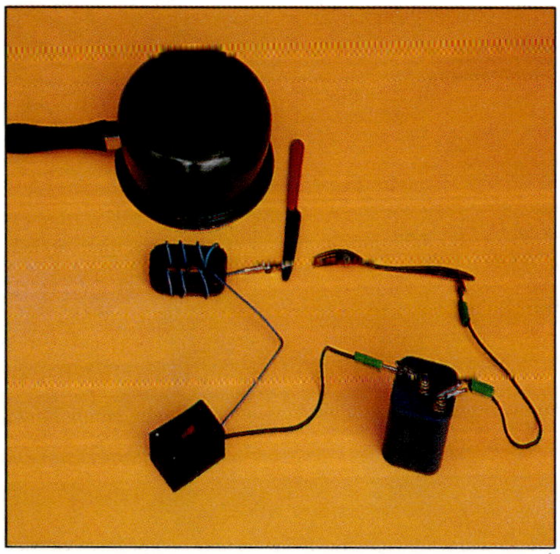

Q1 Why does the clapper hit the gong in a bell?

Q2 What releases the clapper when it has hit the gong?

Q3 The photograph shows a bell made from bits that can be found in a kitchen. Design a bell that uses bits you might find elsewhere in your home. Draw your design.

Relays

You push or pull a switch to make it work.

▶ You could not use a small light switch to operate a large motor in a factory. You would use a relay.

A relay is like the door chime, the armature moves to operate the switch.

Relays are magnetic switches. When the electromagnet is switched on it pulls the armature towards the iron core. The other end of the armature pushes the switch contacts together. When the electromagnet is switched off, the spring pushes the armature away and the switch contacts open again. Relay switches only need a small current flowing through the electromagnet to make them work. The switch circuit is separate from the electromagnet, so the switch can be used to control large currents.

Relays can also be used with small electronic circuits.

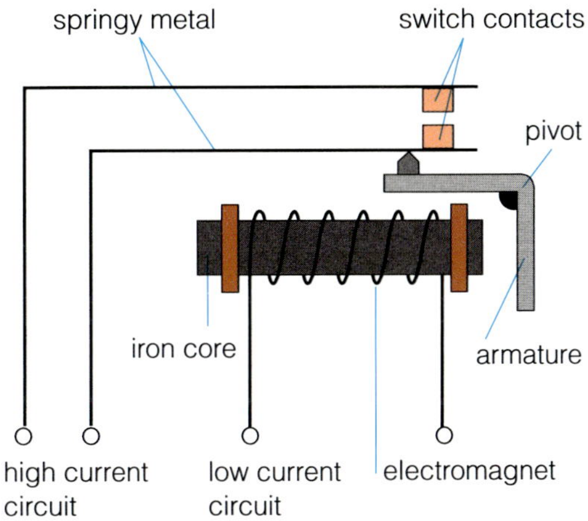

◀ A relay switch can be used in a large greenhouse like this one to turn on the undersoil heaters when the temperature sensor has detected that it is too cold for the plants.

Q1 Write down the sequence of events that happens in the relay switch when the temperature sensor in the greenhouse sends out a signal that it is too cold.

Q2 The rear windscreen heater of a car uses a large current and is switched on by a relay. How does the electricity reach the windscreen heater when it is switched on?

Plotting a magnetic field

In this experiment you are going to plot the **magnetic field** around an electromagnet.

Do not move the magnet once it is set up.

Apparatus

- ☐ sheet of white paper ☐ pencil
- ☐ plotting compass ☐ iron rod
- ☐ sticky tape ☐ Blu-Tack
- ☐ prepared coil ☐ wire strippers
- ☐ crocodile clips
- ☐ low voltage d.c. power supply
- ☐ connecting wires

A Take the 70 turn coil and slide it onto the middle of the iron rod. Use crocodile clips and connecting wires to connect the coil to the power supply. Set it to 1V.

B Stick the paper to the desk with sticky tape. Fix the electromagnet in the middle of the paper with a small piece of Blu-Tack. Draw round it. Put six starting dots near each end of the electromagnet. Switch on the power supply. ▲

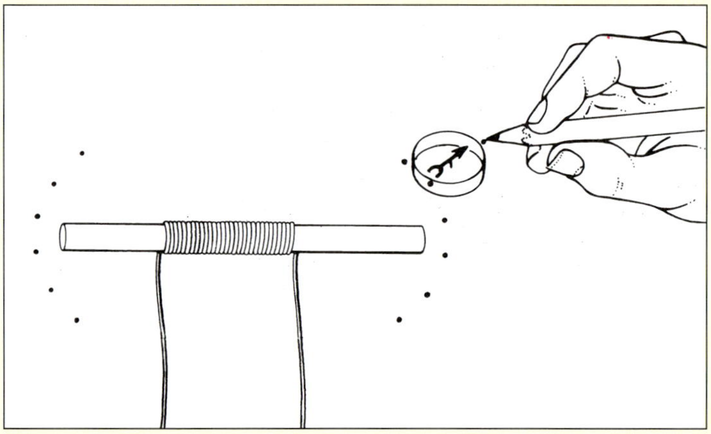

C Place the plotting compass over a dot so it fits by the tail (use the other end of the electromagnet if this doesn't work). Mark another dot by the compass point. ▲

D Place the compass over this new dot and mark another dot by the point of the compass. You can continue the line of dots until it stops or goes off the paper. ▲

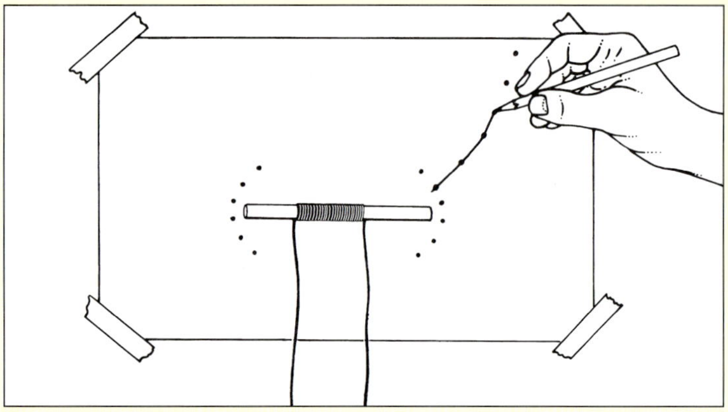

E Join up the line of dots with a smooth pencil line. Choose another starting dot and repeat from **C**. Plot a line of dots from each starting dot. ▲

F When all the starting dots at one end of the magnet are used up, start on the dots at the other end. Place the compass *point* over the starting dot and mark the new dot by the compass *tail*.

Q1 What would the pattern be like if the electromagnet was stronger?

Q2 Do any lines start or end in the middle of the electromagnet?

Q3 What would the pattern be like if the electricity was switched off?

Extension exercise 10 can be used now.

7 Motors

Apparatus

- ☐ ceramic magnets
- ☐ iron U-frame
- ☐ low voltage d.c. power supply
- ☐ clean bare solid copper wires
- ☐ connecting wires
- ☐ crocodile clips
- ☐ clamp and stand (x2)

Electricity, magnets and movement

In this experiment you are going to use magnets and electricity to move things.

A Build this circuit.
The magnets must be put in the U-frame so that they attract each other. ▼

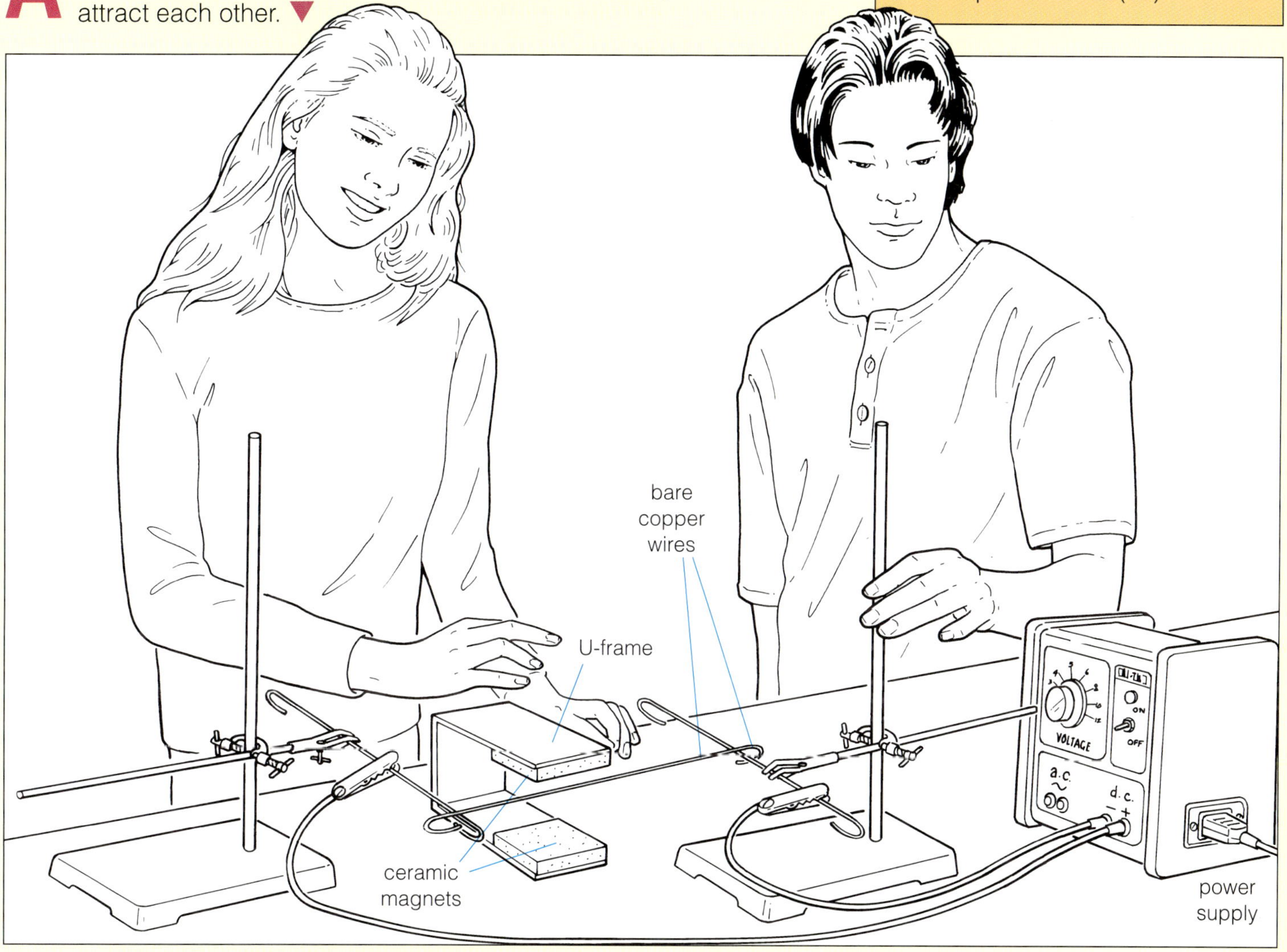

B Set the power supply to 4 volts and switch on.

Q1 What happens when you turn on the power supply?

Q2 How does this effect change if you alter the position of the U-frame and magnets?

Q3 What happens if you change over the + (red) and – (black) connections at the power supply?

Q4 How is the effect altered if the magnets are put in the U-frame so that they repel each other?

Q5 How do you think you can make the effect stronger?
Your teacher may let you try out your ideas.

More movement – motors

An electric motor changes electrical energy into movement energy. The motor has a permanent magnet with an electromagnet (coil) inside that. When the electromagnet is turned on the two fields repel each other and cause movement, and usually the coil spins. A special device is used to get the electricity into the coil, or the wire would become tangled and twisted. It is called a **commutator**. Your teacher will give you a kit to make an electric motor.

Apparatus

- ☐ motor kit
- ☐ low voltage d.c. power pack

A Wind as many turns onto the frame as will fit easily and fix them into place with sticky tape. Leave the two ends with 5 cm free. ▲

B Place the two ceramic magnets in the U-frame to give an attracting field. Put the base into the U-frame and push a split pin into the two holes in the base at either end of the U-frame. ▲

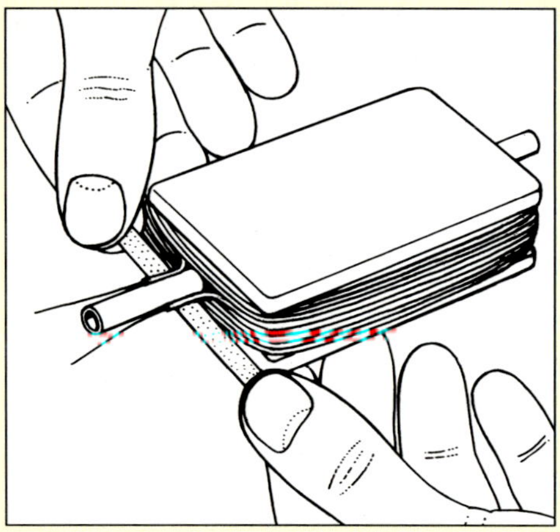

C Strip the plastic off the ends of the wire and fix them in place with sticky tape, with the metal still clear. Place the coil between the magnets and push the thin rod through the hole in the coil and the split pins. ▲

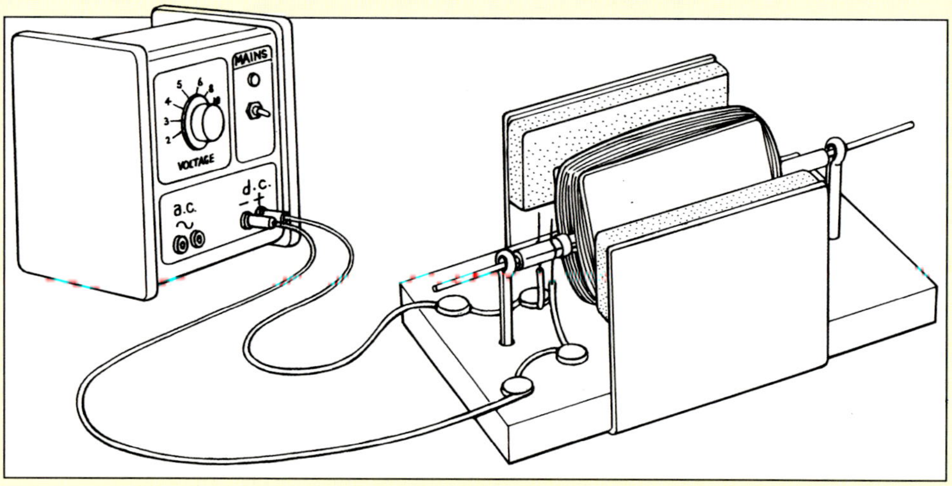

D Two wires 15 cm long, bared at each end, must be fixed to the base by small pins so that when the coil spins the bare ends of the wire touch the wires coming out of the coil. ▲

E Carefully attach the two free ends of the wire to a low voltage power supply set at 4 volts d.c. and switch on. The coil may need a gentle flick to start it spinning.

When the electric current flows round the coil of wire in your motor, the coil becomes an electromagnet. Remember that magnetic forces can repel each other (see page 20).

▶ Each side of the coil is pushed away by the permanent magnets next to them. This makes the coil turn. The commutator makes the current flow in the coil so that the coil is always being pushed round in the same direction.

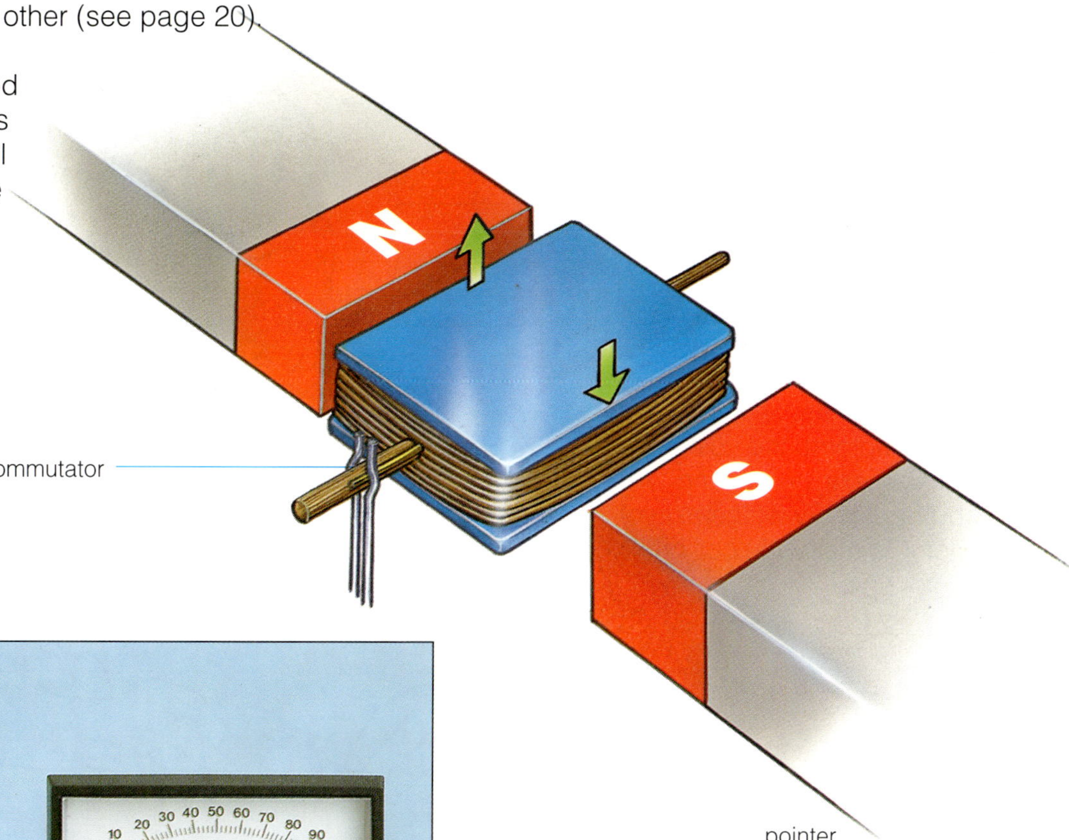

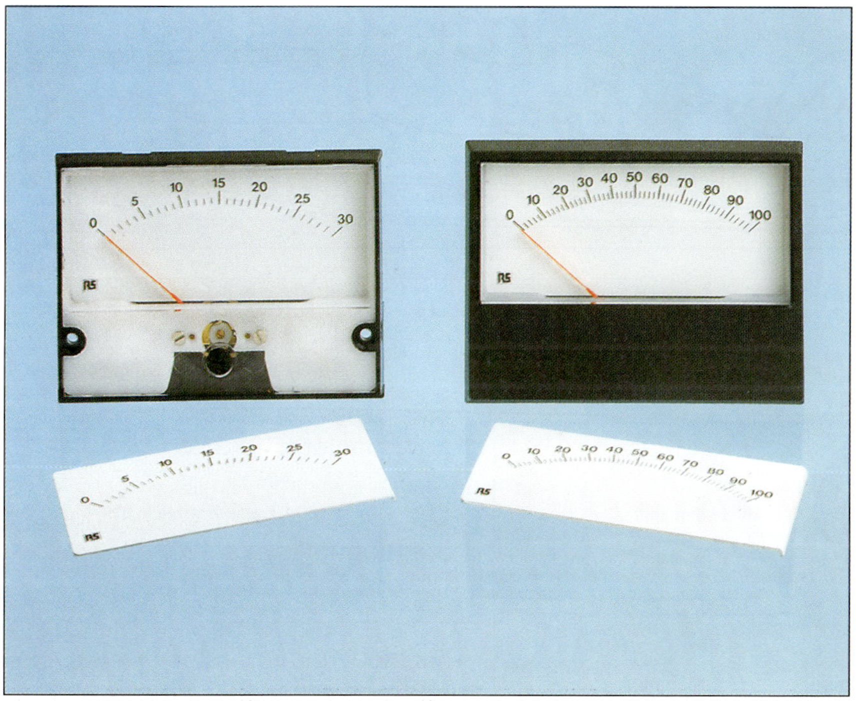

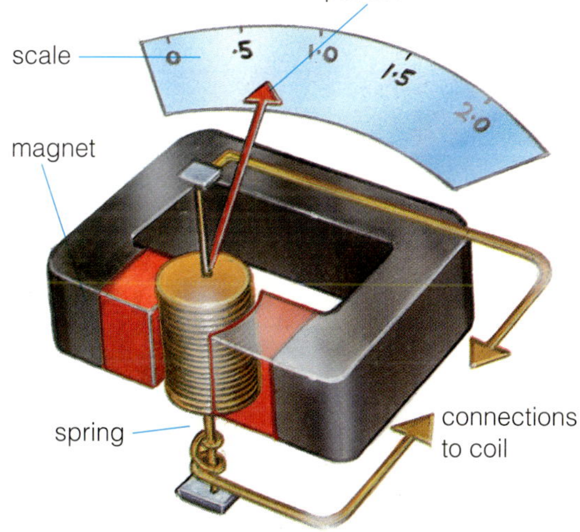

▲ This meter has a coil and permanent magnets. There is a spring attached to the coil. The spring stops the coil spinning. When a current is put through the coil, it turns and pushes against the spring. A small current will push the pointer part way across the scale. A large current will push hard and the pointer will move right across the scale.

Q1 What could you do to the motor to get it to turn faster?

Q2 Find five items in your home that have electric motors inside them. For each item write down.
a what the item is
b what the motor does.

Q3 What makes the electric meter read zero when the electric current is switched off?

Motor or generator?

Most motors will have several coils and a commutator with many sections. Your teacher should be able to show you the inside of a bigger motor.

Apparatus

- ☐ small d.c. motor
- ☐ voltmeter (1 V)
- ☐ crocodile clips
- ☐ connecting wires

Generators are very similar to motors. Let us find out what happens when we spin the coil of the motor.

A Connect the two wires from the motor to the voltmeter using extra wires and crocodile clips. Twist the axle of the motor to make the coil of the motor spin. ▶

Q1 What happens to the meter when the coil spins?

Q2 What happens when the coil spins faster?

Q3 Guess what might happen if the magnets were stronger or if the coil had more turns.

This piece of apparatus is a bicycle **dynamo** (generator) attached to some gears and a handle. ◀

Q4 What happens when the handle is turned quickly?

Q5 Describe what you see as the handle is turned slowly.

Q6 Why do bicycles often have battery lights as well as a dynamo?

8 Making electricity

Electrical induction 1 – a changing effect

Apparatus

- ☐ strong bar magnet
- ☐ prepared coils
- ☐ crocodile clips
- ☐ connecting wires
- ☐ centre reading milliammeter
- ☐ iron rod ☐ sticky tape
- ☐ cardboard tube

Electricity can be made to flow in a circuit using a magnet and movement. This is called **induction**. We say that electricity has been induced into the circuit.

Let us make electricity using a moving magnet. A sensitive meter will show you if any electricity is made.

Q1 Copy this table.

	Meter reading			
	Wire	*30 turn coil*	*70 turn coil*	*70 turn coil with iron rod*
Magnet not moving				
Magnet moving forward				
Magnet moving backward				

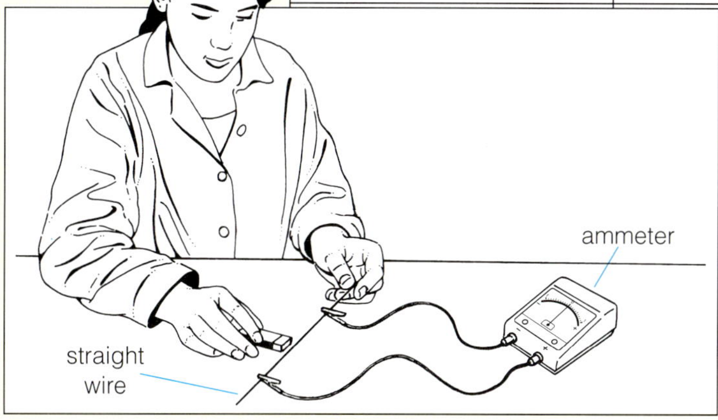

A Build this circuit. Move the magnet quickly while it is close to the wire. Try moving the magnet in different directions. Does the meter show any change? Complete the table. ▲

B Take the 30 turn coil and attach it to the meter. Look at the meter and move the magnet quickly near to and in and out of the coil. Complete the table. ▲

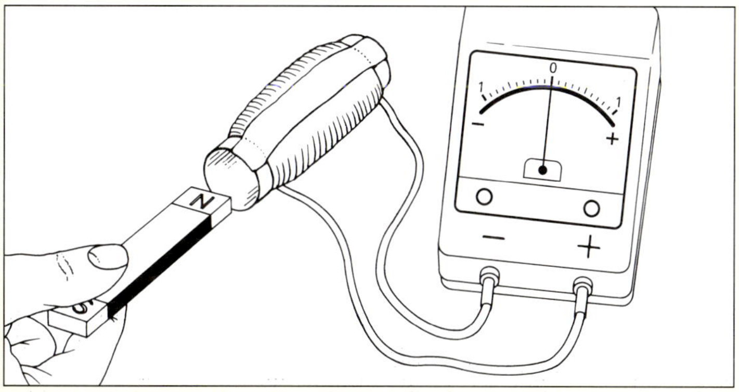

C Take the 70 turn coil and attach it to the meter. Repeat **B**. ▲

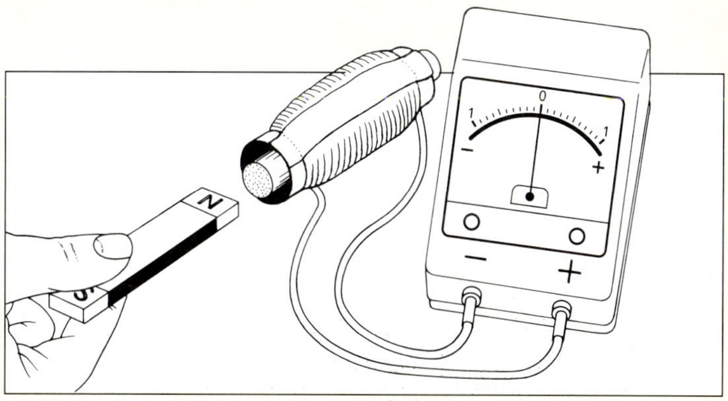

D Place an iron rod into the coil, Repeat **B**. ▲

Q2 What happens to the meter reading if the magnet is moved slowly?

Q3 What happens to the meter reading if the magnet is moved in different directions?

Q4 What happens if the magnet stays still and the coil moves?

Q5 What do you think would be the effect on the meter reading if you used a stronger magnet?

Electrical induction 2

Now let's find out how electricity flowing in one coil can affect another coil.

A '**C**' **core** is a much better shape for getting the magnetism from one coil into the next coil.

Electricity is made (induced) in a circuit only when a magnetic field changes. The magnetic field changes only when the power supply is switched on or off.

Apparatus

- ☐ prepared coils or pieces of insulated wire each 5 metres long
- ☐ centre reading milliammeter
- ☐ iron rod ☐ sticky tape
- ☐ connecting wires
- ☐ 'C' cores and clips
- ☐ low voltage d.c. power supply

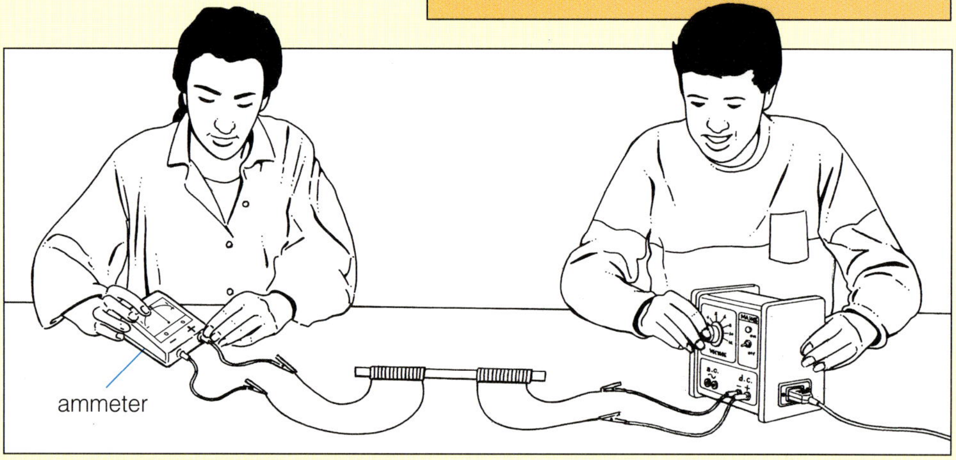

A Wind 50 turns of wire close together onto one end of an iron rod. Fix them in place with sticky tape. Wind another 50 turns on the other end of the rod and fix them in place with sticky tape. ▲

B Build this circuit. Answer **Q1**–**Q3**. Now take out the iron bar and answer **Q1**–**Q3** again. *Switch off* when you have finished. The iron bar lets the magnetism from one coil go into the other coil. ▲

C Unwind the two coils you made and wind 50 turns onto both 'C'-shaped iron cores. Clip them together. Build this circuit. Now repeat **Q1**–**Q3** and then go on to **Q4**.

Q1 What happens to the meter when you switch on the power supply?

Q2 Is there any reading or change on the meter after a few seconds?

Q3 What happens to the meter when you switch off the power supply?

Q4 Are the meter readings bigger, the same or smaller than before?

Transformers

A battery gives a steady flow of electricity. It flows from + to –. The terminals marked ~ or **a.c.** on a power supply give out electricity which is changing all the time. This is called **alternating current** or a.c.

The terminals marked + or – or **d.c.** give out electricity which flows in one direction like a battery. It is called **direct current** or d.c.

Apparatus

- ☐ pieces of insulated wire 5 metres long
- ☐ a.c. voltmeter
- ☐ 12 V bulb and holder
- ☐ 'C' cores and clips
- ☐ low voltage a.c. power supply
- ☐ connecting wires
- ☐ crocodile clips

Let us investigate the effect of a.c. on different coils.

Q1 Copy this table.

Meter reading	Tick brightness of bulb				
	Off	Dim	Normal	Bright	Very bright

A Wind 50 turns onto both 'C' cores and clip them together. Set the power supply to 6 volts. Build this circuit. Connect it to the a.c. terminals. Switch on. Note the meter reading and the brightness of the bulb. Complete the first line of your table. ▲

B Switch off. Unclip the 'C' cores and wind 50 *more* turns of wire onto the coil connected to the bulb. Clip the cores together again and switch on. Note the meter reading and the brightness of the bulb. Complete your table. You have made a simple transformer. A transformer can change a.c. voltages to lower a.c. voltages or to higher a.c. voltages.

Q2 What happened to the reading on the voltmeter when the number of turns of wire increased?

Q3 What happened to the brightness of the bulb when the number of turns of wire increased?

Q4 What might happen if even more turns of wire were put onto the 'C' core?

Alternating and direct current

Batteries and power packs give out direct current (d.c). Mains supplies give out alternating current (a.c.). We can use an oscilloscope to show us the difference between the two.

The trace on the screen shows what the voltage of the electricity supply is doing.

Apparatus

- ☐ oscilloscope ☐ battery
- ☐ battery holder ☐ dynamo
- ☐ connecting wires

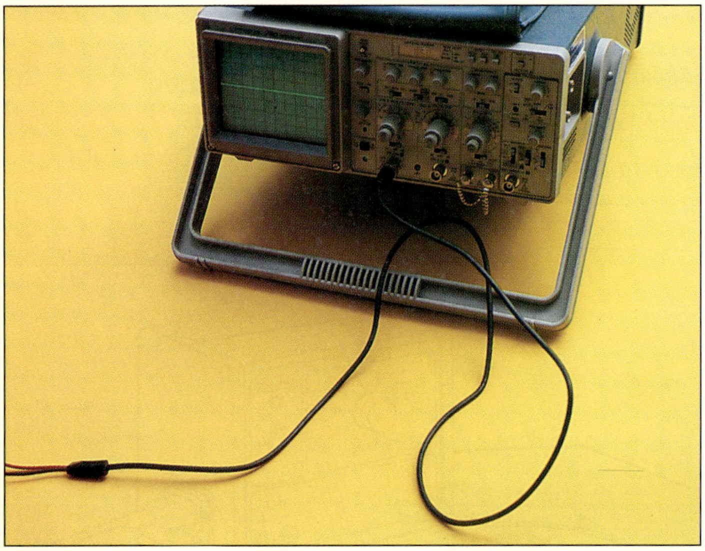

A Set up an oscilloscope so that it has this trace on screen ▲

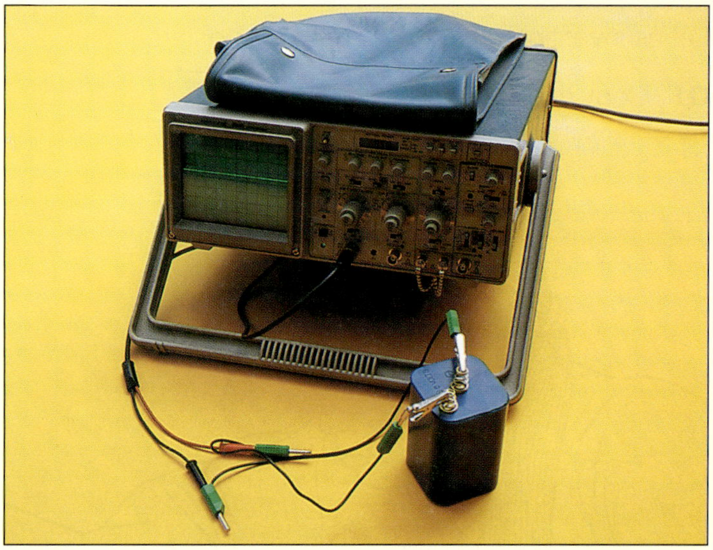

B Touch the clip onto the battery. Note what happens to the trace. ▲

C Turn the battery round and repeat **B**.

D Replace the battery with the dynamo. Turn the handle slowly. Note what you see. ▲

E Turn the handle quickly. Note the difference in the trace.

Q1 For **B**, what happens to the trace? Draw a diagram if it helps.

Q2 How can you tell if a supply is a.c. or d.c., when using an oscilloscope?

Q3 For **D**, what happens to the trace?

Q4 Sometimes a d.c. supply rises and falls slightly. Sketch what the screen trace would look like.

Q5 What might you see an oscilloscope being used for in a hospital?

Using electromagnets and transformers

We need electromagnets

▶ Lots of modern devices use electromagnets. In this photograph you can see the electromagnet inside a radio loudspeaker. Even small personal stereo headphones have a tiny electromagnet in each earpiece.

▶ A car uses a transformer to make large sparks to burn the petrol and make the engine work. It also uses electromagnets in the **alternator**. This is a part of the engine which makes electricity to recharge the battery and run the lights and heater fan.

▲ Large transformers in electricity substations are specially made to change very high voltages down to voltages suitable for our houses. Things like electric keyboards and cassette recorders need even lower voltages. Mains adaptors contain small transformers to change the voltage down further.

Q1 Which part of a telephone uses an electromagnet?

Q2 Why would a car not work if it did not have electromagnets?

Q3 What do transformers in substations do to electricity?

Power stations

▼ Most electricity used in this country is generated in large power stations. They use large generators like the one below. A turbine provides the energy to make the generator turn. Turbines can be driven round by wind or water or steam. The generator that you used on page 30 had magnets that stayed still and a coil that turned in the middle. Large generators keep the coils that generate the electricity still, they are called the **stator coils**. The magnets are rotated inside. Electromagnets are used and these are supplied by a dynamo at the end of the generator. The spinning electromagnets are called the rotor. It is easier to get large amounts of electricity out of a generator if the coils are kept still. A generator that produces alternating current is called an **alternator**.

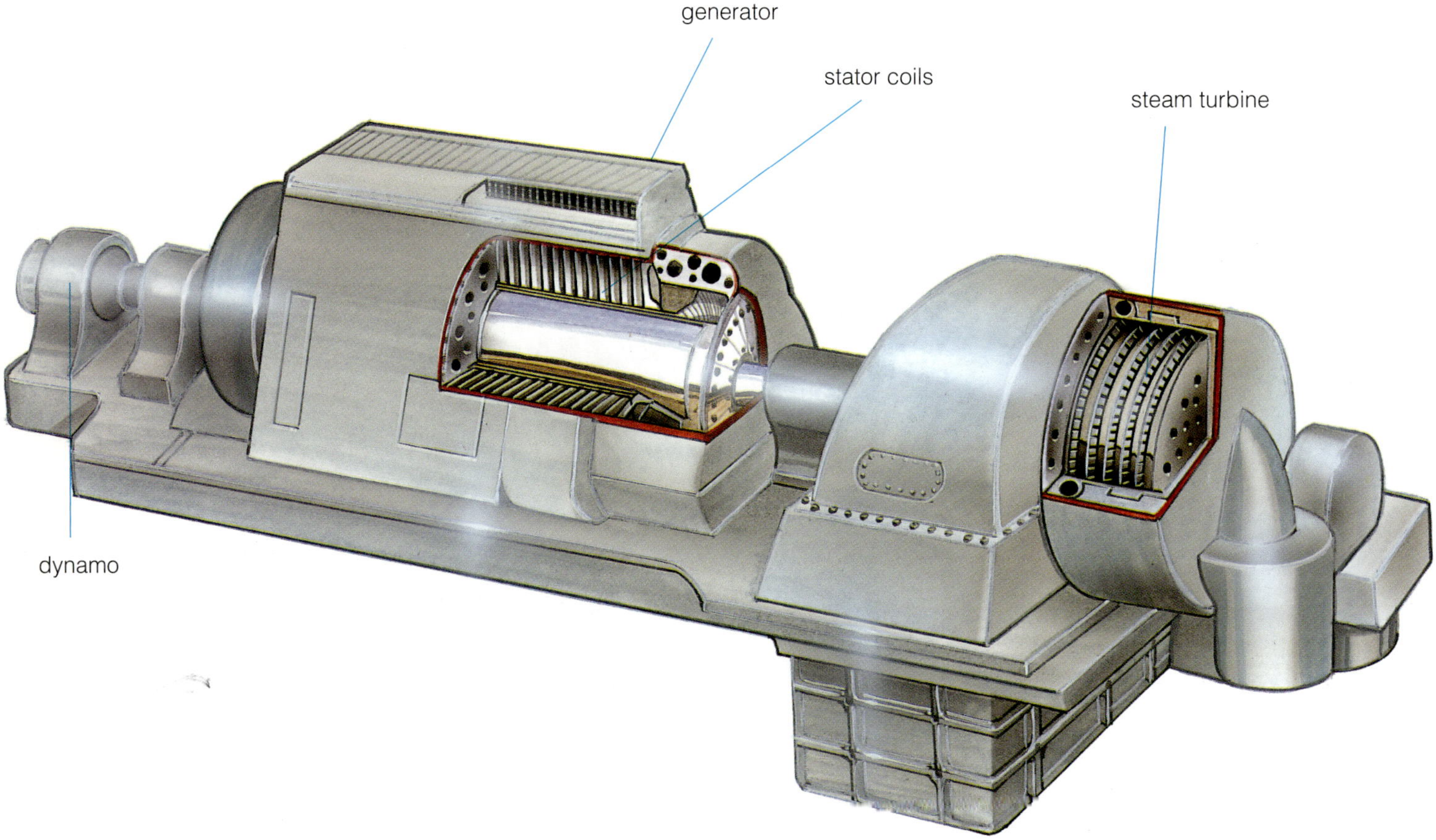

Generators like this can produce electricity at 25 000V with large currents. They have three sets of coils in each generator and each coil produces a separate electrical supply.

Q1 In a generator, what does each of these do:
a turbine?
b stator coils?
c rotor?

Q2 Why is electrical safety very important near to an electrical generator?

Q3 Where does the energy come from to make a large generator work?

How we get our electricity

The generator in the power station makes electricity at a very high voltage. Electricity is carried round the country by the **National Grid**. This is a network of cables hung from large pylons. It is important that the current flowing through the cables is made as small as possible because currents heat the cables and waste energy. To keep the current small you have to increase the voltage. Large transformers are used to increase the voltage and reduce the current. Some parts of the National Grid carry electricity at 400 000V (400kV). Electricity at these voltages has to be carried high above people's heads.

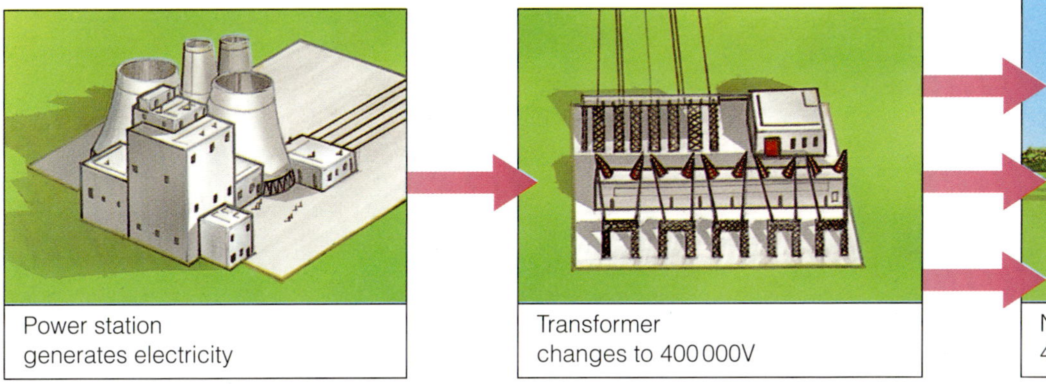

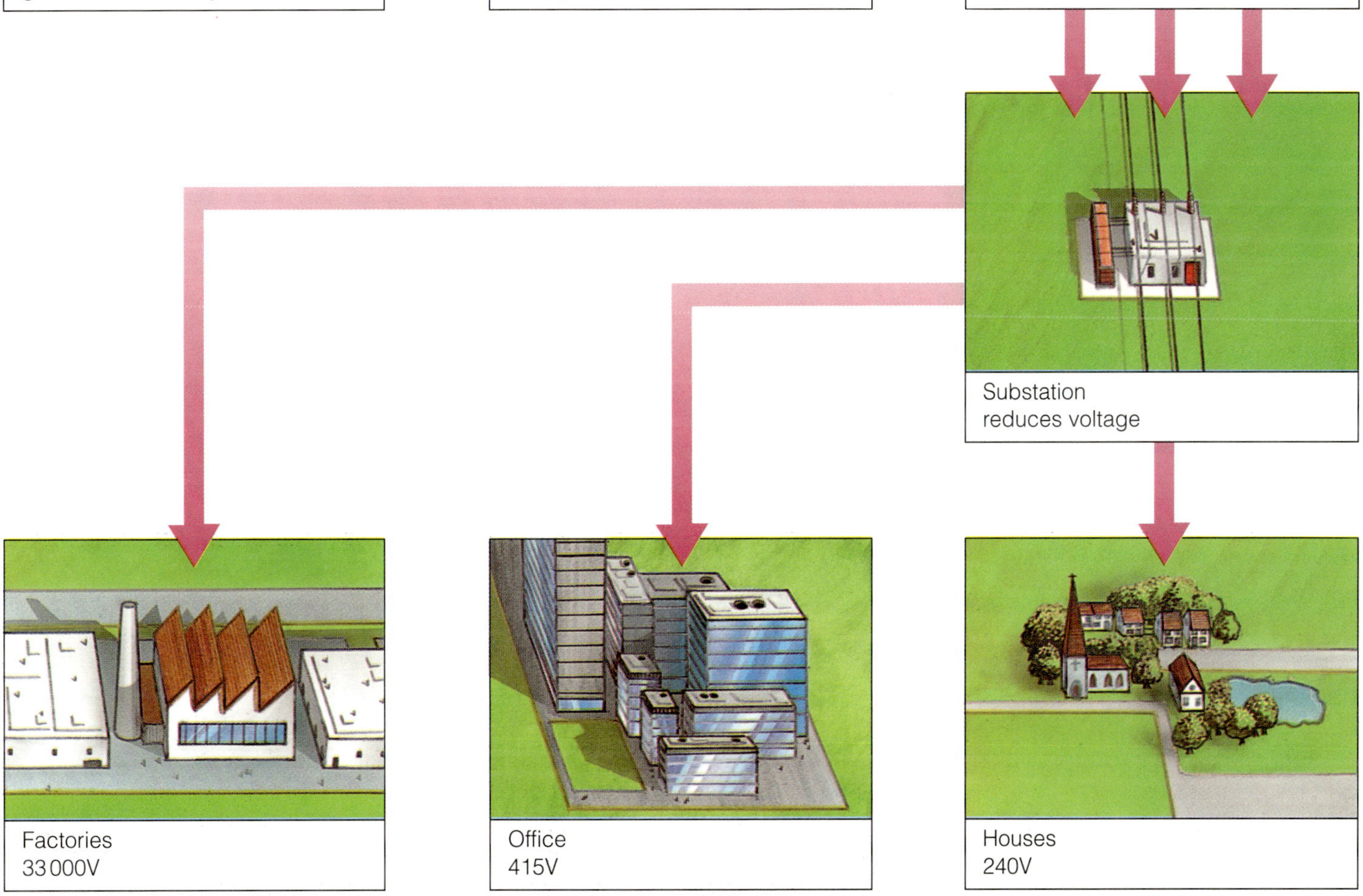

When the electricity gets to where it is used, it is transformed down to safe voltages. Large users like factories have their own transformers and can receive their supply at 33 000 V or 11 000 V. Electrified railways take their supply at 25 000 V. Homes are supplied at a safer 240 V, but even this voltage can be dangerous.

Safety Warning
Electric cables are very dangerous. Never climb pylons or fly kites near them, touch cables or transformers or go near the live rails on railways. A spark of electricity can jump even when you are not touching the cable.

Q1 Use the diagrams given on the copymasters sheet 13 to make a poster illustrating how you get your electricity supply. The poster could be for younger children and should explain the dangers of electricity.

Q2 Why is alternating current used for the supply of electricity?

9 Measuring and paying for electrical energy

How much energy do we use?

A **resistor** controls the amount of electricity flowing in a circuit. This idea was used in the experiments on page 4. A resistor is also used to change electrical energy into heat energy.

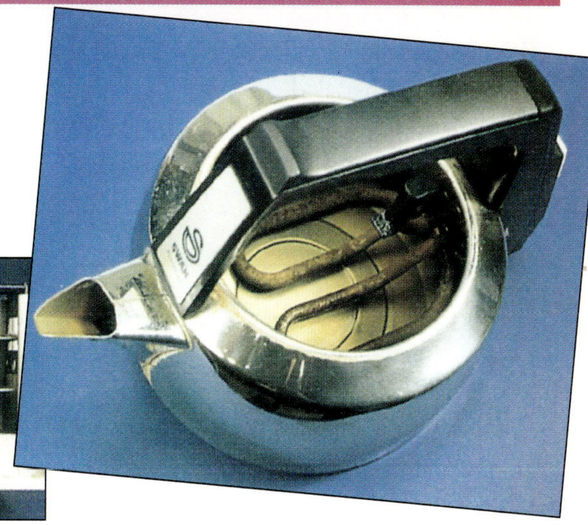

▶ Look at these photographs. They show the heating elements of a kettle and an electric fire. These are used to change electrical energy into heat energy. This change in energy can be measured using a **joulemeter**.

Let's see how much energy is used to heat some water.

Your teacher will build this circuit. ▼

Apparatus

- ☐ low voltage d.c. power supply
- ☐ joulemeter ☐ connecting wires
- ☐ immersion heater
- ☐ metal container for the water

Safety Warning
Immersion heaters get hot! Do not allow them to cool immersed in water.

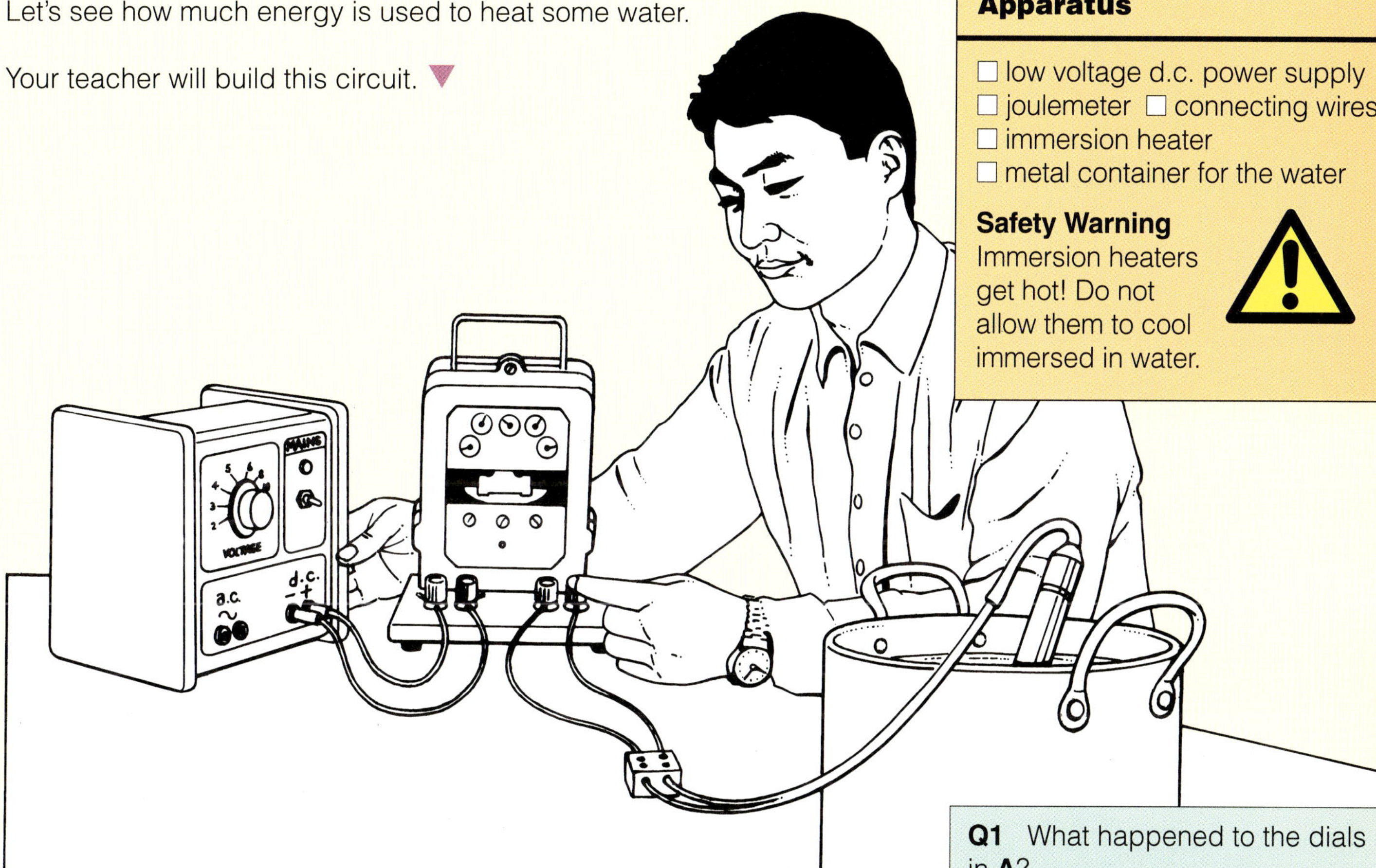

A Note the reading on the joulemeter. This value we will call the old reading.
Switch on the low voltage power supply. Look carefully at the dials on the joulemeter.

B Leave the low voltage power supply switched on for a few minutes. Note the new reading on the joulemeter.

Q1 What happened to the dials in **A**?

Q2 To calculate how much energy has been used subtract the old reading from the new reading. This energy is measured in **joules**.

Extension exercise 11 can be used now.

Electricity isn't free!

Each house has a meter to record the electricity we use so we can be charged for it. It is usually hidden away in a cupboard or under the stairs. There are two main types of meter: 'digital' and 'dial'.

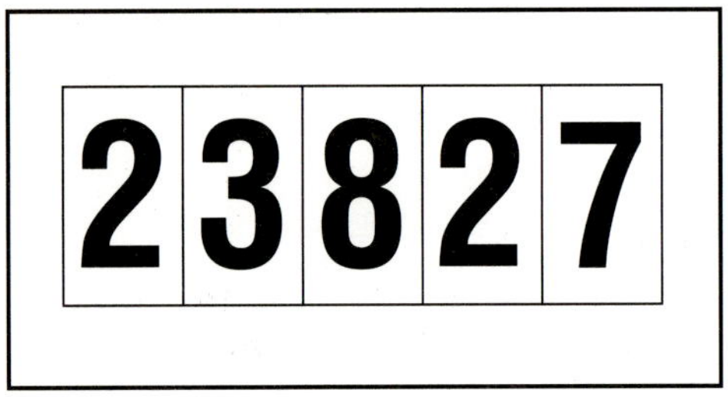

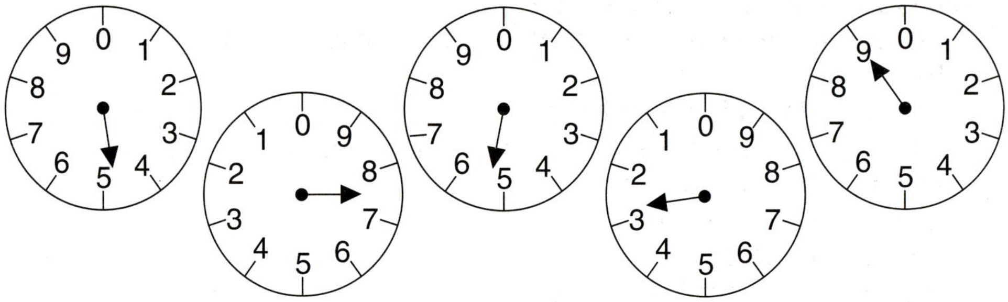

▲ To read the 'digital' type write down the numbers in order. This meter reading is 23827.

▲ To read the 'dial' type write down the number the pointer is at for each dial. If the pointer is not exactly at a number then write the next lower number. This meter reading is 47529.

The meter is usually read every three months or quarter (quarter of a year). To calculate how much electricity has been used you need to know the old reading and subtract it from the new reading. This will give you the electricity used in units of **kilowatt hours**.

▶ The kilowatt hour (kWh) is a unit of energy which is much larger than the joule. The electricity company charge 7.63 pence for each kilowatt hour of electrical energy used. They add a service or standing charge of £10.63 each quarter (1996 prices).

This bill shows:

New reading		Old reading		Units used
15559	–	13628	=	1931 kWh

Cost = 1931 × 7.63p
= 14734 pence
= £147.34
\+ £10.63
= £157.97

SERVING YOU WITH NEW ENERGY

CARTERHATCH LANE ENFIELD EN1 4BW

Mr & Mrs Smith
The 3 Bedroom Semi
Enfield
Middlesex

METER READING THIS TIME	METER READING LAST TIME	UNITS USED	PENCE PER UNIT	AMOUNT £	STANDING CHARGE £	VAT CODE	TOTALS £
15559	13628	1931	7.63	147.34	10.63		157.97

YOUR CUSTOMER NUMBER	YOU CAN PHONE US ON	PERIOD ENDING	AMOUNT DUE NOW
66 9999 4444 66	0181 366 XXXX	19 JUL 96	£ 157.97

C against a meter reading means is your own reading.

E means the meter was not read; you should check this against you meter but any difference will be put right at the next reading.

VAT S = Standard rated M = Mixed rates
O = Zero rated X = Exempt
A = Any VAT included on this charge will have been detailed previously
Registration Number 521 3967 51

YOUR TARIFF IS THE DOMESTIC GENERAL RATE

Extension exercise 12 can be used now.